THE PILGRIM PRAYERBOOK

THE PILGRIM PRAYERBOOK

✠ *David Stancliffe*

continuum
LONDON • NEW YORK

Continuum

The Tower Building, 11 York Road, London, SE1 7NX
370 Lexington Avenue, New York, NY 10017-6503
www.continuumbooks.com

First published 2003

British Library Cataloguing-in-Publication Data
A catalogue record for this book is available from the British Library.

ISBN 0 8264 6694 X (HB Presentation Edition)
ISBN 0 8264 6695 8 (HB Personal Edition)

Designed by Derek Birdsall RDI
Typeset by Omnific
Printed and bound in Great Britain.

Contents

1   Introduction

A Short Guide to the Duties of Church Membership

As baptized and confirmed members of the Church of England, we are called upon to play a full part in its life and witness. That means we should:

Follow the example of Christ in home and daily life, and seek to grow in faith.

Read and study the Bible prayerfully.

Celebrate together in Sunday and weekday worship God's love for the world.

Receive the Holy Communion faithfully and regularly.

Pray daily for the coming of God's kingdom of justice, mercy and peace, seeking to promote the common good by prayer and example.

Express our Christian faith in work and leisure; in the life of our neighbourhood and nation; in our concern for the peoples of the world and the future of the earth.

Dedicate our personal gifts and talents to Christ in the service of the Church and the community.

Give generously for the work of the Church at home and overseas, and for other charitable causes.

Support Christian values, especially relating to marriage, children, family, neighbours and community.

Praying with the Church

The Church has only one prayer – Christ's prayer to the Father. We have no prayer of our own independently of him, and our confidence that our prayer is heard at the throne of God is based on the intimacy of the Son's relationship to the Father. That is why Christian prayer to the Father is characteristically made 'through Jesus Christ our Lord'.

It is this risen and ascended Christ who is seated on the right hand of the Father 'who ever lives to make intercession for us'. In the words of the familiar hymn:

> Look, Father, look on his anointed face,
> And only look on us as found in him.

This means that the Christian who is steeped in Christ's prayer will be praying with the Church. This is why the psalms, so often on the lips of Jesus in the New Testament, have been so important in Christian life and devotion, and why praying through and with scripture occupies such a key place in the history of Christian spirituality and this book.

Praying Christ's prayer means drawing close to him, so that his thoughts become our thoughts, his words our words, his prayer our prayer. At its heart, it is his prayer to the Father – taught in the Lord's Prayer and echoed in the garden of Gethsemane – that 'your will, not mine, be done', and that it be done 'on earth as in heaven'.

So our prayer always begins with blessing God for what he gives, and for being enfolded in the divine love. Within that relationship, we find ourselves drawn more and more into the life of the Trinity. It begins to come naturally that we should pray for his will to be done, and to offer ourselves as the agents of his loving purposes. This, rather than asking God for the things that we want for ourselves, is the true heart of the prayer of the Church in Christ.

The archetype of this prayer is the Church's celebration of the Eucharist, where our offering of ourselves, our souls and bodies, is drawn into the one, perfect offering of the Son to the Father; that is where our fumbling and inarticulate longings are drawn together, cleansed and shaped, and we find ourselves transformed, and given a foretaste of heaven, sharing the life of God himself.

2   Prayers All Christians Pray

The Sign of the Cross

The foundation of our life in Christ is our baptism into his dying and rising. Each time we open our hearts to God in prayer, we recall our baptism. You may trace the sign of the cross, and on entering a church, there may be holy water by the door.

✠ In the name of the Father,
and of the Son,
and of the Holy Spirit. Amen

Based on Matthew 28.19

Our Father

This pattern of praying that Jesus taught his disciples has been at the heart of the Church's prayer from earliest days. Our prayer is to enter the Son's prayer to the Father, that his will, not ours, be done.

Our Father, who art in heaven,
hallowed be thy name;
thy kingdom come;
thy will be done;
on earth as it is in heaven.
Give us this day our daily bread.
And forgive us our trespasses,
as we forgive those who trespass against us.
And lead us not into temptation;
but deliver us from evil.
For thine is the kingdom,
the power and the glory,
for ever and ever. Amen.

Based on Matthew 6.9 –15

The Apostles' Creed

*The confession of faith rehearsed by candidates for baptism in the undivided Church is ·
the Apostles' Creed. The Latin name for a creed is 'symbolum': a creed is a standard of
faith in a shorthand form, like a coat of arms or a flag, which can easily be recognized
and to which we can pledge allegiance.*

I believe in God, the Father almighty,
creator of heaven and earth.

I believe in Jesus Christ, his only Son, our Lord,
who was conceived by the Holy Spirit,
born of the Virgin Mary
suffered under Pontius Pilate,
was crucified, died, and was buried;
he descended to the dead.
On the third day he rose again;
he ascended into heaven,
he is seated at the right hand of the Father,
and he will come to judge the living and the dead.

I believe in the Holy Spirit,
the holy catholic Church,
the communion of saints,
the forgiveness of sins,
the resurrection of the body,
and the life everlasting.
Amen.

Jesus' Summary of the Law

The first commandment is this:
'Hear, O Israel, the Lord our God is the only God.
You shall love the Lord your God with all your heart,
and with all your soul, and with all your mind,
    and with all your strength.'
The second is this:
'You shall love your neighbour as yourself.'
There is no commandment greater than these.

Mark 12.29 – 31

The Beatitudes

The fundamental Jewish tradition of prayer is to bless God for what he has done, and in that context to ask his blessing on particular people, or groups or objects. The Beatitudes show Jesus applying this directly to the poor, the weak and the vulnerable with the prayer that the values of this world may be reversed in God's kingdom.

Blessed are the poor in spirit,
for theirs is the kingdom of heaven.

Blessed are those who mourn,
for they shall be comforted.

Blessed are the meek,
for they shall inherit the earth.

Blessed are those who hunger and thirst after righteousness,
for they shall be satisfied.

Blessed are the merciful,
for they shall obtain mercy.

Blessed are the pure in heart,
for they shall see God.

Blessed are the peacemakers,
for they shall be called children of God.

Blessed are those who suffer persecution for righteousness' sake,
for theirs is the kingdom of heaven.

Matthew 5.3–12

The Jesus Prayer

This short prayer, based on the prayer of the sinner whom Jesus compared favourably with the Pharisee, is repeated over and over again with each slow breath in the Orthodox tradition.

> Lord Jesus Christ, Son of God
> have mercy on me, a sinner.

cf. Luke 18.13b

Gloria Patri

The praises of God the Holy Trinity, used at the opening of worship and after each psalm and canticle.

> Glory to the Father, and to the Son, and to the Holy Spirit:
> As it was in the beginning is now, and shall be for ever. Amen.

3   Daily Prayer

From earliest times, Christians have prayed at certain points in the day, using the dawn and the dusk, midday and bedtime, as markers to peg their prayer for their immediate concerns into God's eternal work of redemption and renewal. That fourfold pattern evolved in time into a daily recollection of God's engagement with us in the incarnation of his Son, focused in the four Canticles in the opening chapters of St Luke's Gospel.

These four Gospel canticles have become the traditional climax to daily prayer at morning, noon, evening and night. In Morning Prayer, the Church looks forward to what glimpses of God's kingdom the new day will bring. At noon we are reminded of the message that the angel brought to Mary requesting her co-operation, and like her practise saying 'yes' to God. In the evening we look back on the day and rejoice that God has indeed 'put down the mighty from their seat' and are challenged: have we helped that to happen today? And as we go to bed, we are helped, like old Simeon in the Temple, to recognize the Light of the World, and ask God to help us let go, that we may rest in peace.

This traditional shape is visible in the daily pattern that follows, helping to root our prayer within the prayer of the whole Church from the time of the apostles till now. More important still is that we enter the eternal prayer of Christ to the Father, which is why each set Order of prayer includes verses of the psalms, which formed such a significant part of Christ's prayer. Praying to the Father in words that Christ used, using ourselves the prayers of praise and lament, anxiety and rejoicing that unite us in a continuous stream of human supplication from his time to ours, binds us together in seeking to do God's will. For at the heart of our prayer are the words Jesus himself taught us: 'Thy kingdom come, thy will be done, on earth as it is in heaven.'

3.1   The Canticles of Luke's Gospel

Morning Prayer

Benedictus (The Song of Zechariah)

Blessed be the Lord the God of Israel,
Who has come to his people and set them free.

He has raised up for us a mighty Saviour,
born of the house of his servant David.

Through his holy prophets God promised of old
to save us from our enemies,
From the hands of all that hate us,

To show mercy to our ancestors,
And to remember his holy covenant.

This was the oath God swore to our father Abraham:
to set us free from the hands of our enemies,

Free to worship him without fear,
holy and righteous in his sight
all the days of our life.

And you, child, shall be called the prophet of the Most High,
For you will go before the Lord to prepare his way,

To give his people knowledge of salvation
by the forgiveness of all their sins.

In the tender compassion of our God
The dawn from on high shall break upon us,

To shine on those who dwell in darkness and the shadow of death,
And to guide our feet into the way of peace.

Luke 1.68 – 79

Glory to the Father and to the Son
And to the Holy Spirit;
as it was in the beginning is now
And shall be for ever. Amen.

Midday Prayer

The Salutation of Mary

Hail Mary, full of grace,
the Lord is with you.
Blessed are you among women,
and blessed is the fruit of your womb.

Luke 1.26b, 42b

Evening Prayer

Magnificat (The Song of Mary)

My soul proclaims the greatness of the Lord,
my spirit rejoices in God my Saviour;
he has looked with favour on his lowly servant.

From this day all generations will call me blessed;
The Almighty has done great things for me
and holy is his name.

He has mercy on those who fear him,
from generation to generation.

He has shown strength with his arm
And has scattered the proud in their conceit,

Casting down the mighty from their thrones
And lifting up the lowly.

He has filled the hungry with good things
And sent the rich away empty.

He has come to the aid of his servant Israel,
to remember his promise of mercy,

The promise made to our ancestors,
to Abraham and his children for ever.

Luke 1.46 –55

Glory to the Father and to the Son
And to the Holy Spirit;
as it was in the beginning is now
And shall be for ever. Amen.

Night Prayer

Nunc dimittis (The Song of Simeon)

> Now, Lord, you let your servant go in peace:
> your word has been fulfilled.
>
> My own eyes have seen the salvation
> which you have prepared in the sight of every people;
>
> A light to reveal you to the nations
> And the glory of your people Israel.

Luke 2.29 −32

> Glory to the Father and to the Son
> And to the Holy Spirit;
> as it was in the beginning is now
> And shall be for ever. Amen.

3.2 Morning Prayer

The traditional heart of Morning Prayer is the praise of God at the dawning of the day for the resurrection, and our new life in Christ. The week still has the natural shape articulated in the Jewish tradition by the days of creation in the first creation narrative in Genesis which culminates in the celebration of the Sabbath. For Christians, the celebration of the first day of the week as a weekly memorial of the resurrection has given shape to our worship, and each day starts with praising God for the new creation, for the rising of the Sun of Righteousness.

The continuity of our praise with the prayer of Jesus himself is emphasized in our continuing use of the psalms, which, then as now, are at the heart of Jewish worship. In using the psalms we join the unbroken chain of worship, singing the praises of God as we come before him in every kind of mood. Some psalms praise God for what he has done in rescuing his people; some plead with him not to forget his people, as he appears to have done; some are prayers for protection and mercy; some are written out of a sense of despair and isolation; some express anger, hurt and resentment; some pray for peace or prosperity; some seem almost nauseatingly self-righteous and others are caught in wonder at the majesty and splendour of God's overarching purposes. All human emotion is there, and in praying the psalms we are caught into the age-old pattern of turning our attention from preoccupation with ourselves and our needs towards God, what he is doing and where he needs our help.

The Gospel canticle at Morning Prayer, the Benedictus, is the climax of this longing to be taking our part in recognizing the signs of God's kingdom, and helping it to happen.

> Blessed be the Lord the God of Israel,
> who has come to his people and set them free …
> free to worship him without fear,
> holy and righteous in his sight
> all the days of our life.
>
> In the tender compassion of our God
> the dawn from on high shall break upon us,
> to shine on those who dwell in darkness and the shadow of death,
> and to guide our feet into the way of peace.

It is in this spirit that we rise to greet the dawning day, and tune our hearts and minds to the beat of God's love, that his will may be done and his kingdom come today and every day.

Morning Prayer on Sunday

O Lord, open my lips
and my mouth shall proclaim your praise.

Glory to the Father and to the Son and to the Holy Spirit;
as it was in the beginning is now and shall be for ever. Amen.

Praise of God for the resurrection of Christ

Blessed are you, Lord God our redeemer;
to you be praise and glory for ever.
From the waters of chaos you drew forth the world,
and in your great love, fashioned us in your image.
Now, through the deep waters of death
you have brought your people to new birth
by raising your Son to life in triumph.
May we, the first fruits of your new creation,
rejoice in this new day you have made;
may Christ your light ever dawn in our hearts
as we offer you our sacrifice of thanks and praise:
Blessed be God for ever,
Father, Son, and Holy Spirit.

Verses from Psalm 118

The Lord is my strength and my song,
and he has become my salvation.

I shall not die, but live
and declare the works of the Lord.

Open to me the gates of righteousness,
that I may enter and give thanks to the Lord.

I will give thanks to you, for you have answered me
and have become my salvation.

The stone which the builders rejected
has become the chief cornerstone.

This is the Lord's doing,
and it is marvellous in our eyes.

This is the day that the Lord has made;
we will rejoice and be glad in it.

One of these short readings may be used.

Week 1

> In the beginning, God created the heavens and the earth.
> The earth was without form and void and darkness was on
> face of the deep, and the Spirit of God was moving over the face
> of the waters. And God said, 'Let there be light'; and there
> was light. And God saw that the light was good.
>
> *Genesis 1.1 –3*

Week 2

> We know that Christ, being raised from the dead, will never die
> again; death no longer has dominion over him. The death he
> died, he died to sin, once for all; but the life he lives, he lives to
> God. So you also must consider yourselves dead to sin and alive
> to God in Christ Jesus.
>
> *Romans 6.9–11*

Week 3

> If you have been raised with Christ, seek the things that are
> above, where Christ is, seated at the right hand of God. Set your
> minds on things that are above, not on things that are on the
> earth. For you have died, and your life is hid with Christ in God.
> When Christ who is your life is revealed, then you also will be
> revealed with him in glory.
>
> *Colossians 3.1–4*

Week 4

> I handed on to you as of first importance what I in turn had
> received: that Christ died for our sins in accordance with the
> scriptures, and that he was buried, and that he was raised on the
> third day in accordance with the scriptures, and that he appeared
> to Peter, then to the twelve. If Christ has not been raised, your
> faith is futile and you are still in your sins. But in fact Christ has
> been raised from the dead, the first fruits of those who have
> fallen asleep. For since by man came death, by man has come
> also the resurrection of the dead; for as in Adam all die, so also
> in Christ shall all be made alive.
>
> *1 Corinthians 15.3–5,17,20–22*

> Behold, I stand at the door and knock; if anyone hears my voice and
> opens the door, I will come in to them and eat with them, and they
> with me.

Revelation 3.20—22

or

> Jesus said to her, 'I am the resurrection and the life; whoever believes
> in me, though they die, yet shall they live, And whoever lives and
> believes in me shall never die. Do you believe this?' She said to him,
> 'Yes, Lord; I believe that you are the Christ, the Son of God, he who
> is coming into the world.'

John 11.25—27

Reflection on the reading concludes with:

> Awake, O sleeper, and arise from the dead,
> and Christ shall give you light.

The Gospel Canticle: The Song of Zecharaiah

✠ Blessed be the Lord the God of Israel,
who has come to his people and set them free.

He has raised up for us a mighty Saviour,
born of the house of his servant David.

Through his holy prophets God promised of old
to save us from our enemies,
from the hands of all that hate us,

To show mercy to our ancestors,
and to remember his holy covenant.

This was the oath God swore to our father Abraham:
to set us free from the hands of our enemies,

Free to worship him without fear,
holy and righteous in his sight
all the days of our life.

And you, child, shall be called the prophet of the Most High,
for you will go before the Lord to prepare his way,

To give his people knowledge of salvation
by the forgiveness of all their sins.

In the tender compassion of our God
the dawn from on high shall break upon us,

To shine on those who dwell in darkness and the shadow of death,
and to guide our feet into the way of peace.

Luke 1.68—79

Glory to the Father and to the Son and to the Holy Spirit;
as it was in the beginning is now and shall be for ever. Amen.

On Sundays the Church prays

∗ for the Church throughout the world, that we may proclaim the risen Christ

∗ for God's world, that we may care for the fragile creation

∗ for those who are afraid, that they may find new hope and life in Christ

O God,
through the mighty resurrection of your Son, Jesus Christ,
you have delivered us from the power of darkness
and brought us into the kingdom of your love;
grant that, as he was raised from the dead
so we may walk in newness of life
and seek those things that are above;
where with you, Father, and the Holy Spirit,
he is alive and reigns,
now and for ever. Amen.

Morning Prayer concludes with the Our Father, and this ending:

May the Lord bless us this day, preserve us from all evil,
and keep us in life eternal. Amen.

Morning Prayer on Monday

O Lord, open my lips
and my mouth shall proclaim your praise.

Glory to the Father and to the Son and to the Holy Spirit;
as it was in the beginning is now and shall be for ever. Amen.

Praise of God for the gift of his Spirit

Blessed are you, creator God,
to you be glory and praise for ever.
Your Spirit moved over the face of the waters
to bring light and life to your creation.
Pour out your Spirit on us this day
that we may walk as children of light
and by your grace reveal your presence.
Blessed be God for ever,
Father, Son, and Holy Spirit.

Verses from Psalm 103

Bless the Lord, O my soul,
and all that is within me bless his holy name.

Bless the Lord, O my soul,
and forget not all his benefits;

Who forgives all your sins
and heals all your infirmities;

Who redeems your life from the Pit
and crowns you with faithful love and compassion;

Who satisfies you with good things,
so that your youth is renewed like an eagle's.

Bless the Lord, all you works of his,
in all places of his dominion;
bless the Lord, O my soul.

One of these short readings may be used.

Week 1

God said, 'Let us make man in our image, according to our likeness, and let them have dominion over the fish of the sea, and over the birds of the air, and over the cattle, and over all the wild animals of the earth, and over every creeping thing that creeps upon the earth.' So God created man in his image, in the image of God he created him, male and female he created them. God blest them and said to them, 'Be fruitful and multiply, and fill the earth and subdue it; and have dominion over the fish of the sea and over the birds of the air and over every living thing that moves upon the earth.'

Genesis 1.26–28

Week 2

Since we are justified by faith, we have peace with God through our Lord Jesus Christ, through whom we have obtained access to this grace in which we stand; and we boast in our hope of sharing the glory of God. And not only that, but we also boast in our sufferings, knowing that suffering produces endurance, and endurance produces character, and character produces hope, and hope does not disappoint us, because God's love has been poured into our hearts through the Holy Spirit that has been given to us.

Romans 5.1–5

Week 3

There are varieties of gifts but the same Spirit; and there are varieties of service but the same Lord; and there are varieties of activities but it is the same God who inspires them all in everyone. To each is given the manifestation of the Spirit for the common good. For just as the body is one and has many members, and all the members of the body, though many, are one body, so it is with Christ. For in the one Spirit we were all baptized into one body – Jews or Greeks, slaves or free – and we were all made to drink of one spirit.

1 Corinthians 12.4–7,12–13

The Lord said: I will pour out my spirit on all flesh; your sons and your daughters shall prophesy, your old men shall dream dreams and your young men shall see visions. Even upon the menservants and maidservants in those days, I will pour out my spirit.

Joel 2.28–29

On any Monday

On the last day of the feast, the great day, Jesus stood up and proclaimed, 'If any one thirst, let him come to me and drink. He who believes in me, as the scripture has said, out of his heart shall flow rivers of living water.'

John 7.37–38

or

The Spirit of the Lord is upon me, because he has anointed me to preach good news to the poor.

Luke 4.18a

Reflection on the reading concludes with:

Come, Holy Spirit, fill the hearts of your people
and kindle in us the fire of your love.

The Gospel Canticle: The Song of Zecharaiah

✠ Blessed be the Lord the God of Israel,
who has come to his people and set them free.

He has raised up for us a mighty Saviour,
born of the house of his servant David.

Through his holy prophets God promised of old
to save us from our enemies,
from the hands of all that hate us,

To show mercy to our ancestors,
and to remember his holy covenant.

This was the oath God swore to our father Abraham:
to set us free from the hands of our enemies,

Free to worship him without fear,
holy and righteous in his sight
all the days of our life.

And you, child, shall be called the prophet of the Most High,
for you will go before the Lord to prepare his way,

To give his people knowledge of salvation
by the forgiveness of all their sins.

In the tender compassion of our God
the dawn from on high shall break upon us,

To shine on those who dwell in darkness and the shadow of death,
and to guide our feet into the way of peace.

Luke 1.68–79

Glory to the Father and to the Son and to the Holy Spirit;
as it was in the beginning is now and shall be for ever. Amen.

On Mondays the Church prays

✳ that those who wait on God may be renewed by the Spirit

✳ that the media may pursue and communicate the truth

✳ that all who travel may journey safely

O God, forasmuch as without you
we are not able to please you;
mercifully grant that your Holy Spirit
may in all things direct and rule our hearts;
through Jesus Christ your Son our Lord,
who is alive and reigns with you,
in the unity of the Holy Spirit,
one God, now and for ever.

Morning Prayer concludes with the Our Father, and this ending:

May the Lord bless us this day, preserve us from all evil,
and keep us in life eternal. Amen.

O Lord, open my lips
and my mouth shall proclaim your praise.

Glory to the Father and to the Son and to the Holy Spirit;
as it was in the beginning is now and shall be for ever. Amen.

Praise of God for the coming of his Kingdom

Blessed are you, Sovereign God of all,
to you be praise and glory for ever.
In your tender compassion
the dawn from on high is breaking upon us
to dispel the lingering shadows of night.
As we look for your coming among us this day,
open our eyes to behold your presence
and strengthen our hands to do your will,
that the world may rejoice and give you praise.
Blessed be God for ever,
Father, Son and Holy Spirit.

Verses from Psalm 24

The earth is the Lord's and all that fills it,
the compass of the world and all who dwell therein.

For he has founded it upon the seas
and set it firm upon the rivers of the deep.

'Who shall ascend the hill of the Lord,
or who can rise up in his holy place?'

'Those who have clean hands and a pure heart,
who have not lifted up their soul to an idol,
nor sworn an oath to a lie;

'They shall receive a blessing from the Lord,
a just reward from the God of their salvation.'

Such is the company of those who seek him,
of those who seek your face, O God of Jacob.

Lift up your heads, O gates;
be lifted up, you everlasting doors;
and the King of glory shall come in.

'Who is this King of glory?'
'The Lord of hosts, he is the King of glory.'

One of these short readings may be used.

Week 1

Now it is full time for you to awake from sleep, for salvation is nearer
to us now than when we first believed; the night is far gone, the day is
at hand. Let us then cast aside the works of darkness and put on the
armour of light. Put on the Lord Jesus Christ and make no provision
for the flesh, to gratify its desires.

Romans 13.11–12,14

Week 2

Take up the whole armour of God, so that you may be able to
withstand on that evil day, and having done everything, to stand firm.
Stand, therefore, having girded your loins with truth, and having put
on the breastplate of righteousness, and having shod your feet with the
equipment of the gospel of peace; above all, taking the shield of faith,
with which you will be able to quench all the flaming arrows of the
evil one. Take the helmet of salvation and the sword of the Spirit,
which is the word of God. Pray in the Spirit at all times in every
prayer and supplication.

Ephesians 6.13–18a

Week 3

The word of the Lord came to Elijah, saying, 'Go out and stand
on the mountain before the Lord, for the Lord is passing by.' Now
there was a great wind, so strong that it was splitting mountains and
breaking rocks in pieces before the Lord; but the Lord was not in
the wind. And after the wind, an earthquake; but the Lord was not
in the earthquake. And after the earthquake, a fire; but the Lord
was not in the fire. And after the fire, a still small voice.

1 Kings 19.11–12

Jesus said, 'When the Son of Man comes in his glory, and all the angels with him, then he will sit on the throne of his glory. The king will say to those at his right hand, "Come, O blessèd of my Father, inherit the kingdom prepared for you from the foundation of the world; for I was hungry and you gave me food, I was thirsty and you gave me drink, I was a stranger and you welcomed me, I was naked and you clothed me, I was sick and you visited me, I was in prison and you came to me."'

Matthew 25.31,34–36

On any Tuesday

The Kingdom of heaven is like a merchant in search of fine pearls, who, on finding one of great value, went and sold all that he had and bought it.

Matthew 13.45

or

Whoever wishes to become great among you must be your servant, and whoever wishes to be first among you must be servant of all. For the Son of Man came not to be served but to serve, and to give his life as a ransom for many.

Mark 10.42–45

Reflection on the reading concludes with:

In your tender compassion, O God
the dawn from on high shall break upon us.

The Gospel Canticle: The Song of Zecharaiah

✠ Blessed be the Lord the God of Israel,
who has come to his people and set them free.

He has raised up for us a mighty Saviour,
born of the house of his servant David.

Through his holy prophets God promised of old
to save us from our enemies,
from the hands of all that hate us,

To show mercy to our ancestors,
and to remember his holy covenant.

This was the oath God swore to our father Abraham:
to set us free from the hands of our enemies,

Free to worship him without fear,
holy and righteous in his sight
all the days of our life.

And you, child, shall be called the prophet of the Most High,
for you will go before the Lord to prepare his way,

To give his people knowledge of salvation
by the forgiveness of all their sins.

In the tender compassion of our God
the dawn from on high shall break upon us,

To shine on those who dwell in darkness and the shadow of death,
and to guide our feet into the way of peace.

Luke 1.68–79

Glory to the Father and to the Son and to the Holy Spirit;
as it was in the beginning is now and shall be for ever. Amen.

✳ that the nations and their leaders may be subject to God's rule

✳ that the victims of injustice may find freedom and hope

✳ that the Church may champion the rights of the poor and oppressed

O Lord,
you have set before us the great hope that your kingdom
    shall come on earth,
and have taught us to pray for its coming;
give us grace to discern the signs of it dawning,
and to work for the perfect day
when your will shall be done on earth as it is in heaven;
through Jesus Christ our Lord.

Percy Dearmer (1867-1936)

Morning Prayer concludes with the Our Father, and this ending:

May the Lord bless us this day, preserve us from all evil, and keep us in life eternal. Amen.

Morning Prayer on Wednesday

O Lord, open my lips
and my mouth shall proclaim your praise.

Glory to the Father and to the Son and to the Holy Spirit;
as it was in the beginning is now and shall be for ever. Amen.

Praise of God for the Incarnation of Christ

Blessed are you, Sovereign God, creator of all,
to you be glory and praise for ever.
You founded the earth in the beginning
and the heavens are the work of your hands.
As we rejoice in the gift of your presence among us
let the light of your love always shine in our hearts,
and your praises ever be on our lips:
Blessed be God for ever,
Father, Son, and Holy Spirit.

Verses from Psalm 8

O Lord our governor,
how glorious is your name in all the world!

Your majesty above the heavens is praised
out of the mouths of babes at the breast.

When I consider your heavens, the work of your fingers,
the moon and the stars that you have ordained,

What is man, that you should be mindful of him;
the son of man, that you should seek him out?

You have made him little lower than the angels
and crown him with glory and honour.

You have given him dominion over the works of your hands
and put all things under his feet.

O Lord our governor,
how glorious is your name in all the world!

One of these short readings may be used.

Week 1

> Now the word of the Lord came to me, saying, 'Before I formed you in the womb, I knew you. And before you were born I consecrated you. I appointed you a prophet to the nations.' Then I said, 'Ah, Lord God! Truly I do not know how to speak, for I am only a youth.' But the Lord said to me, 'Do not say "I am only a youth", for you shall go to all to whom I send you, and you shall speak whatever I command you. Do not be afraid of them for I am with you to deliver,' says the Lord.

Jeremiah 1.4–6

Week 2

> Jesus said, 'You are the light of the world. A city set on a hill cannot be hid. No one after lighting a lamp puts it under a bushel but on the lampstand and it gives light to all in the house. In the same way, let your light so shine before others that they may see your good works and glorify your Father who is in heaven.'

Matthew 5.14–16

Week 3

> John summoned two of his disciples and sent them to the Lord to ask, 'Are you the one who is to come or are we to wait for another?' And Jesus answered them, 'Go and tell John what you have seen and heard: the blind receive their sight, the lame walk, the lepers are cleansed, the deaf hear, the dead are raised, the poor have good news brought to them. And blessèd is anyone who takes no offence at me.'

Luke 7.19,22–23

Week 4

> How beautiful on the mountains are the feet of the messenger who announces peace, who brings good news, who announces salvation, who says to Zion, 'Your God reigns.' Listen! Your sentinels lift up their voices, together they sing for joy; for in plain sight they see the return of the Lord to Zion. Break forth into singing, you ruins of Jerusalem, for the Lord has comforted his people, he has redeemed Jerusalem.

Isaiah 52.7–9

On any Wednesday

Jesus spoke to the Pharisees, saying, 'I am the light of the world. Whoever follows me will never walk in darkness but will have the light of life.'

John 8.12

or

You know the grace of our Lord Jesus Christ, that though he was rich, yet for your sakes he became poor, so that, by his poverty, you might become rich.

2 Corinthians 8.9

Reflection on the reading concludes with:

From the rising of the sun to its setting
Your glory is proclaimed in all the world.

The Gospel Canticle: The Song of Zecharaiah

✠ Blessed be the Lord the God of Israel,
who has come to his people and set them free.

He has raised up for us a mighty Saviour,
born of the house of his servant David.

Through his holy prophets God promised of old
to save us from our enemies,
from the hands of all that hate us,

To show mercy to our ancestors,
and to remember his holy covenant.

This was the oath God swore to our father Abraham:
to set us free from the hands of our enemies,

Free to worship him without fear,
holy and righteous in his sight
all the days of our life.

And you, child, shall be called the prophet of the Most High,
for you will go before the Lord to prepare his way,

To give his people knowledge of salvation
by the forgiveness of all their sins.

In the tender compassion of our God
the dawn from on high shall break upon us,

To shine on those who dwell in darkness and the shadow of death,
and to guide our feet into the way of peace.

Luke 1.68–79

Glory to the Father and to the Son and to the Holy Spirit;
as it was in the beginning is now and shall be for ever. Amen.

* that the Church may be the agent of God's peace

* for children, especially refugees and the vulnerable, and for those
who care for them

* for the fearful and lonely, that they may know the presence of Christ

Almighty God,
you have created the heavens and the earth
and made us in your own image:
teach us to discern your hand in all your works
and your likeness in all your children;
through Jesus Christ your Son our Lord,
who with you and the Holy Spirit reigns supreme over all things,
now and for ever.

Morning Prayer concludes with the Our Father, and this ending:

May the Lord bless us this day, preserve us from all evil,
and keep us in life eternal. Amen.

Morning Prayer on Thursday

O Lord, open my lips
and my mouth shall proclaim your praise.

Glory to the Father and to the Son and to the Holy Spirit;
as it was in the beginning is now and shall be for ever. Amen.

Praise of God for the presence of Christ

Blessed are you, Sovereign God, King of the nations,
to you be glory and praise for ever.
From the rising of the sun to its setting
your name is proclaimed in all the world.
As the Sun of Righteousness dawns in our hearts,
anoint our lips with the seal of your Spirit
that we may witness to your gospel
and sing your praise in all the world:
Blessed be God for ever,
Father, Son, and Holy Spirit.

Verses from Psalm 34

I will bless the Lord at all times;
his praise shall ever be in my mouth.

I sought the Lord and he answered me
and delivered me from all my fears.

Look upon him and be radiant
and your faces shall not be ashamed.

This poor soul cried, and the Lord heard me
and saved me from all my troubles.

The angel of the Lord encamps around those who fear him
and delivers them.

O taste and see that the Lord is gracious;
blessed is the one who trusts in him.

One of these short readings may be used.

Week 1

> How are they to call on one in whom they have not believed?
> And how are they to believe in one of whom they have never heard?
> And how are they to hear without a preacher? And how are they to
> preach him unless they are sent? As it is written, 'How beautiful
> are the feet of those who bring good news!'

Romans 10.14–15

Week 2

> Moses said, 'I call heaven and earth to witness against you today that
> I have set before you life and death, blessing and curse. Therefore,
> choose life, that you and your descendants may live, loving the Lord
> your God, obeying his voice and holding fast to him; for that means
> life to you and length of days.

Deuteronomy 30.19–20

Week 3

> As many of you as were baptized into Christ have put on Christ.
> There is no longer Jew or Greek, there is no longer slave or free,
> there is no longer male and female; for you are all one in Christ Jesus.
> And if you are Christ's, then you are Abraham's offspring, heirs
> according to the promise.

Galatians 3.27–29

Week 4

> If anyone is in Christ, there is a new creation. The old has passed
> away, behold, the new has come. All this is from God, who
> through Christ reconciled us to himself and gave us the ministry of
> reconciliation; that is, God was in Christ reconciling the world to
> himself, not counting their trespasses against them, and entrusting to
> us the message of reconciliation. So we are ambassadors for Christ.

2 Corinthians 5.17–20a

Jesus said, 'I am the living bread that came down from heaven. Whoever eats of this bread will live for ever; and the bread that I will give for the life of the world is my flesh.'

John 6.51

or

Jesus said, 'You did not choose me, but I chose you, and appointed you, that you should go and bear fruit, and bear it abundantly.'

John 15.16

Reflection on the reading concludes with:

Fear not, for I have redeemed you.
I have called you by name; you are mine.

The Gospel Canticle: The Song of Zecharaiah

✠ Blessed be the Lord the God of Israel,
who has come to his people and set them free.

He has raised up for us a mighty Saviour,
born of the house of his servant David.

Through his holy prophets God promised of old
to save us from our enemies,
from the hands of all that hate us,

To show mercy to our ancestors,
and to remember his holy covenant.

This was the oath God swore to our father Abraham:
to set us free from the hands of our enemies,

Free to worship him without fear,
holy and righteous in his sight
all the days of our life.

And you, child, shall be called the prophet of the Most High,
for you will go before the Lord to prepare his way,

To give his people knowledge of salvation
by the forgiveness of all their sins.

In the tender compassion of our God
the dawn from on high shall break upon us,

To shine on those who dwell in darkness and the shadow of death,
and to guide our feet into the way of peace.

Luke 1.68—79

Glory to the Father and to the Son and to the Holy Spirit;
as it was in the beginning is now and shall be for ever. Amen.

On Thursdays the Church prays

* for the unity of the Church, and for all ministers of the gospel

* for those who work for peace and reconciliation

* for the healing of the sick in mind and body, and for the medical profession

O Lord, we beseech you mercifully to hear the prayers
of your people who call upon you;
and grant that they may both perceive and know
what things they ought to do,
and also may have grace and power faithfully to fulfil them;
through Jesus Christ your Son our Lord,
who is alive and reigns with you,
in the unity of the Holy Spirit,
one God, now and for ever.

Morning Prayer concludes with the Our Father, and this ending:

May the Lord bless us this day, preserve us from all evil,
and keep us in life eternal. Amen.

Morning Prayer on Friday

O Lord, open my lips
and my mouth shall proclaim your praise.

Glory to the Father and to the Son and to the Holy Spirit;
as it was in the beginning is now and shall be for ever. Amen.

Praise of God for light in the darkness of sin

Blessed are you, God of compassion and mercy,
to you be praise and glory for ever.
In the darkness of our sin,
your light breaks forth like the dawn
and your healing springs up for deliverance.
As we rejoice in the gift of your saving help,
sustain us with your bountiful Spirit
and open our lips to sing your praise:
Blessed be God for ever,
Father, Son, and Holy Spirit.

Verses from Psalm 51

Have mercy on me, O God, in your great goodness;
according to the abundance of your compassion blot out my offences.

Wash me thoroughly from my wickedness
and cleanse me from my sin.

For I acknowledge my faults
and my sin is ever before me.

Cast me not away from your presence
and take not your holy spirit from me.

Give me again the joy of your salvation
and sustain me with your gracious spirit;

Then shall I teach your ways to the wicked
and sinners shall return to you.

One of these short readings may be used.

Week 1

Abraham bound his son Isaac, and laid him on the altar, on top of the wood. Then he reached out his hand and took the knife to slay his son. But the angel of the Lord called to him from heaven and said, 'Abraham, Abraham! Do not lay your hand on the boy or do anything to him, for now I know that you fear God, since you have not withheld your son, your only son, from me.'

Genesis 22.9b–12

Week 2

While we were yet helpless, at the right time Christ died for the ungodly. Indeed, rarely will anyone die for a righteous person – though perhaps for a good person someone might actually dare to die. But God proves his love for us in that while we were still sinners Christ died for us.

Romans 5.6–8

Week 3

I have been crucified with Christ, and it is no longer I who live but it is Christ who lives in me. And the life I now live in the flesh I live by faith in the Son of God, who loved me and gave himself for me.

Galatians 2.20

Week 4

The love of Christ urges us on, because we are convinced that one has died for all; therefore all have died. And he died for all so that those who live might live no longer for themselves but for him who died and was raised for them.

2 Corinthians 5.14–15

On any Friday

Unless a grain of wheat falls into the earth and dies, it remains alone; but if it dies, it bears a rich harvest.

John 12.24

Jesus said, 'I, when I am lifted up from the earth, will draw all people to myself.'

John 12.32

Reflection on the reading concludes with:

Come, let us return to the Lord,
for our God will richly pardon.

The Gospel Canticle: The Song of Zecharaiah

✠ Blessed be the Lord the God of Israel,
who has come to his people and set them free.

He has raised up for us a mighty Saviour,
born of the house of his servant David.

Through his holy prophets God promised of old
to save us from our enemies,
from the hands of all that hate us,

To show mercy to our ancestors,
and to remember his holy covenant.

This was the oath God swore to our father Abraham:
to set us free from the hands of our enemies,

Free to worship him without fear,
holy and righteous in his sight
all the days of our life.

And you, child, shall be called the prophet of the Most High,
for you will go before the Lord to prepare his way,

To give his people knowledge of salvation
by the forgiveness of all their sins.

In the tender compassion of our God
the dawn from on high shall break upon us,

To shine on those who dwell in darkness and the shadow of death,
and to guide our feet into the way of peace.

Luke 1.68–79

Glory to the Father and to the Son and to the Holy Spirit;
as it was in the beginning is now and shall be for ever. Amen.

On Fridays the Church prays

∗ for the suffering Church, and for courage to take up the cross of Christ

∗ for the victims and perpetrators of violence, and all who are falsely accused

∗ for healing within the wounds of Christ

Almighty God,
who called your Church to bear witness
that you were in Christ reconciling the world to yourself:
help us to proclaim the good news of your love,
that all who hear it may be drawn to you;
through him who was lifted up on the cross,
and reigns with you in the unity of the Holy Spirit,
one God, now and for ever.

Morning Prayer concludes with the Our Father, and this ending:

May the Lord bless us this day, preserve us from all evil,
and keep us in life eternal. Amen.

Morning Prayer on Saturday

O Lord, open my lips
and my mouth shall proclaim your praise.

Glory to the Father and to the Son and to the Holy Spirit;
as it was in the beginning is now and shall be for ever. Amen.

Praise of God for the glory that surrounds us as we journey

Blessed are you, Sovereign God,
ruler and judge of all;
to you be praise and glory for ever.
In the darkness of this age that is passing away,
may the glory of your kingdom which the saints enjoy
surround our steps as we journey on.
May we reflect the light of your glory this day
and so be made ready to come into your presence.
Blessed be God for ever,
Father, Son, and Holy Spirit.

Verses from Psalm 95

O come, let us sing to the Lord;
let us heartily rejoice in the rock of our salvation.

Let us come into his presence with thanksgiving
and be glad in him with psalms.

For the Lord is a great God
and a great king above all gods.

Come, let us worship and bow down
and kneel before the Lord our Maker.

For he is our God;
we are the people of his pasture and the sheep of his hand.

One of these short readings may be used.

Week 1

Jacob dreamed that there was a ladder set up on the earth, the top of it reaching to heaven; and the angels of God were ascending and descending on it. And the Lord stood beside him and said, 'I am the Lord, the God of Abraham your father and the God of Isaac; the land on which you lie I will give to you and to your offspring.' Then Jacob woke from his sleep and said, 'Surely the Lord is in this place, and I did not know it!' And he was afraid and said, 'How awesome is this place! This is none other than the house of God, and this is the gate of heaven.'

Genesis 28.12–13,16–17

Week 2

Therefore, since we are surrounded by so great a cloud of witnesses, let us also lay aside every weight and the sin that clings so closely, and let us run with perseverance the race that is set before us, looking to Jesus the pioneer and perfecter of our faith, who for the sake of the joy that was set before him endured the cross, despising the shame, and is seated at the right hand of the throne of God.

Hebrews 12.1–4

Week 3

Not that I have already obtained this or have already reached the goal, but I press on to make it my own, because Christ Jesus has made me his own. Belovèd, I do not consider that I have made it my own, but this one thing I do: forgetting what lies behind and straining forward to what lies ahead, I press on toward the goal for the prize of the upward call of God in Christ Jesus.

Philippians 3.12–14

Week 4

So we do not lose heart. Though our outer nature is wasting away, our inner nature is being renewed every day. For this slight momentary affliction is preparing for us an eternal weight of glory beyond all comparison, because we look not to the things that are seen but to the things that are unseen; for the things that are seen are transient, but the things that are unseen are eternal.

2 Corinthians 4.16–18

Thomas said to him, 'Lord, we do not know where you are going; how can we know the way?' Jesus said to him, 'I am the way, and the truth, and the life; no one comes to the Father, but by me.'

John 14.5–6

or

Many waters cannot quench love,
neither can the floods drown it.

Song of Solomon 8.7

Reflection on the reading concludes with:

You will guide us with your counsel, O God,
and after, receive us with glory.

The Gospel Canticle: The Song of Zecharaiah

✠ Blessed be the Lord the God of Israel,
   who has come to his people and set them free.

He has raised up for us a mighty Saviour,
born of the house of his servant David.

Through his holy prophets God promised of old
to save us from our enemies,
from the hands of all that hate us,

To show mercy to our ancestors,
and to remember his holy covenant.

This was the oath God swore to our father Abraham:
to set us free from the hands of our enemies,

Free to worship him without fear,
holy and righteous in his sight
all the days of our life.

And you, child, shall be called the prophet of the Most High,
for you will go before the Lord to prepare his way,

To give his people knowledge of salvation
by the forgiveness of all their sins.

In the tender compassion of our God
the dawn from on high shall break upon us,

To shine on those who dwell in darkness and the shadow of death,
and to guide our feet into the way of peace.

Luke 1.68–79

Glory to the Father and to the Son and to the Holy Spirit;
as it was in the beginning is now and shall be for ever. Amen.

✳ that God's people may live as citizens of heaven

✳ that the nations of the world may live in peace and harmony

✳ that the dying may come to know the joy of resurrection

Almighty and everlasting God,
increase in us your gift of faith
that, forsaking what lies behind
and reaching out to that which is before,
we may run the way of your commandments
and win the crown of everlasting joy;
through Jesus Christ your Son our Lord,
who is alive and reigns with you,
in the unity of the Holy Spirit,
one God, now and for ever.

Morning Prayer concludes with the Our Father, and this ending:

May the Lord bless us this day, preserve us from all evil,
and keep us in life eternal. Amen.

3.3　Memorial of the Incarnation

The Angelic Salutation is traditionally prayed at midday. Pausing and praying this ancient pattern of reflecting on scripture brings us face to face with God's call to do his will — to say yes to his initiative.

The Angel of the Lord brought tidings to Mary
and she conceived by the Holy Spirit.

Hail Mary, full of grace, the Lord is with you.
Blessèd are you among women,
and blessèd is the fruit of your womb, Jesus.
Holy Mary, Mother of God, pray for us sinners,
now, and at the hour of our death. Amen.

'Behold, the handmaid of the Lord;
let it be to me according to your word.'

Hail Mary, full of grace, the Lord is with you.
Blessèd are you among women,
and blessèd is the fruit of your womb, Jesus.
Holy Mary, Mother of God, pray for us sinners,
now, and at the hour of our death. Amen.

The Word was made flesh
and dwelt among us.

Hail Mary, full of grace, the Lord is with you.
Blessèd are you among women,
and blessèd is the fruit of your womb, Jesus.
Holy Mary, Mother of God, pray for us sinners,
now, and at the hour of our death. Amen.

Pray for us, O holy Mother of God,
that we may be made worthy of the promises of Christ.

Let us pray

> We beseech you, O Lord,
> to pour your grace into our hearts;
> that as we have known the incarnation
> of your Son Jesus Christ
> by the message of an angel,
> so by his ✠ cross and passion
> we may be brought to the glory of his resurrection;
> through Jesus Christ our Lord. Amen.

3.4 Evening Prayer

As giving thanks for the risen Christ was at the centre of prayer at the dawning of the day in the early Church, so the heart of evening prayer was the celebration of the evening light as the lamps were lit at sundown. The tradition of blessing God for the evening light persisted until the time of the poet and parson, George Herbert, who wrote:

> Another old Custome there is of saying, when light is brought in, God send us the light of heaven; and the Parson likes this very well; neither is he afraid of praising, or praying to God at all times, but is rather glad of opportunities to do them. Light is a great Blessing, and as great as food, for which we give thanks.

When Archbishop Thomas Cranmer devised Evening Prayer in the Book of Common Prayer, he drew together elements of Vespers and Compline, which is why Evensong has both the Magnificat and the Nunc Dimittis, which properly belongs to Compline. In this book, Evening Prayer begins with the Blessing of Light and has the Magnificat, the Song of Mary, as its Gospel Canticle. Compline comes at the very end of the day, with its prayers for surrender to sleep and safe-keeping reaching a climax in the Nunc Dimittis, the Song of Simeon.

An Order for Evening Prayer

The Blessing of Light

The Lord is my light and my salvation:
my God shall make my darkness to be bright.

May the light and peace of Jesus Christ be with us.

A lamp or candle may be lit.

Blessed are you, Lord God, creator of day and night:
to you be praise and glory for ever.
As darkness falls you renew your promise
to reveal among us the light of your presence.
May your Word be a lantern to my feet
and a light upon my path,
that I may walk as a child of light
and sing your praise throughout the world:
Blessed be God for ever,
Father, Son, and Holy Spirit.

The Song of Light, Phos hilaron, may follow.

O gladdening light,
of the holy glory of the immortal Father
heavenly, holy, blessed,
O Jesus Christ.

Now that we have come to the setting of the sun
and see the evening light
we give praise to God,
Father, Son and Holy Spirit.

Worthy are you at all times
to be worshipped with holy voices,
O Son of God and giver of life:
therefore all the world glorifies you.

Verses from Psalm 141 may follow, and incense may be burned.

Let my prayer rise before you as incense,
the lifting up of my hands as the evening sacrifice.

O Lord, I call to you; come to me quickly;
hear my voice when I cry to you.
Set a watch before my mouth, O Lord,
and guard the door of my lips;

Let my prayer rise before you as incense,
the lifting up of my hands as the evening sacrifice.

Let not my heart incline to any evil thing;
let me not be occupied in wickedness with evildoers.
But my eyes are turned to you, Lord God;
in you I take refuge; do not leave me defenceless.

Let my prayer rise before you as incense,
the lifting up of my hands as the evening sacrifice.

This prayer may follow after some silence.

As our evening prayer rises before you, O God,
so may your mercy come down upon us
to cleanse our hearts
and set us free to sing your praise
now and for ever. Amen.

The Word of God

Some verses of a psalm and a short reading may follow, or you may use another pattern of Bible reading and reflection. Or you may move straightaway to the Gospel Canticle and Prayer.

On Sundays

Bless the Lord, O my soul.
O Lord my God, how excellent is your greatness!

You are clothed with majesty and honour,
wrapped in light as in a garment.

The sun knows the time for its setting.
You make darkness that it may be night.

I will sing to the Lord as long as I live;
I will make music to my God while I have my being.

Psalm 104.1,2,21b,22a,35

Fear not, I am the first and the last, and the living one;
I died, and behold I am alive for evermore, and I have the keys of
Death and Hades.

Revelation 1.17b–18

On Mondays

O Lord, how manifold are your works!
In wisdom you have made them all;
the earth is full of your creatures.

When you send forth your spirit, they are created,
and you renew the face of the earth.

May the glory of the Lord endure for ever;
may the Lord rejoice in his works.

Psalm 104.26,32,33

The fruit of the Spirit is love, joy, peace, patience, kindness, goodness,
faithfulness, self-control. If we live by the Spirit, let us walk by the
Spirit.

Galatians 5.22,23a, 25

Show us your mercy, O Lord.
and grant us your salvation.

Truly, his salvation is near to those who fear him,
that his glory may dwell in our land.

Mercy and truth are met together,
righteousness and peace have kissed each other;

Truth shall spring up from the earth
and righteousness look down from heaven.

Righteousness shall go before him
and direct his steps in the way.

Psalm 85.7,9—11,13

Christ Jesus was in the form of God, but did not count equality with
God a thing to be grasped, but emptied himself, taking the form of a
servant, and was born in human likeness.

Philippians 2.6—7

On Wednesdays

I love you, O Lord my strength;
The Lord is my crag, my fortress and my deliverer.

In my distress I called upon the Lord
and cried out to my God for help.

He heard my voice in his temple
and my cry came to his ears.

He parted the heavens and came down
and thick darkness was under his feet.

For you will save a lowly people
and bring down the high looks of the proud.

You also shall light my candle;
the Lord my God shall make my darkness to be bright.

Psalm 18.1,6,7,10,28,29

We proclaim not ourselves, but Christ Jesus as Lord, and ourselves as your servants for Jesus' sake. For it is the God who said, 'Let light shine out of darkness,' who has shone in our hearts to give the knowledge of the glory of God in the face of Jesus Christ.

2 Corinthians 4.5–6

On Thursdays

Sing to the Lord a new song;
sing to the Lord, all the earth.

Sing to the Lord and bless his name;
tell out his salvation from day to day.

Declare his glory among the nations
and his wonders among all peoples.

O worship the Lord in the beauty of holiness;
let the whole earth tremble before him.

Tell it out among the nations that the Lord is king.
He has made the world so firm that it cannot be moved;
he will judge the peoples with equity.

Psalm 96.1–3,9–10

You are a chosen race, a royal priesthood, a holy nation, God's own people, in order that you may proclaim the wonderful deeds of him who called you out of darkness into his marvellous light.

1 Peter 2.9

On Fridays

As the deer longs for the water brooks,
so longs my soul for you, O God.

My soul is athirst for God, even for the living God;
when shall I come before the presence of God?

Why are you so full of heaviness, O my soul,
and why are you so disquieted within me?

O put your trust in God;
for I will yet give him thanks,
who is the help of my countenance, and my God.

Psalm 42.1–2,6–7

We preach Christ crucified, a stumbling block to the Jews and folly to the Gentiles, but to those who are called, both Jews and Greeks, Christ the power of God and the wisdom of God. For the foolishness of God is wiser than men, and the weakness of God is stronger than men.

1 Corinthians 1.23—25

On Saturdays

I am always with you;
you hold me by my right hand.

You will guide me with your counsel
and afterwards receive me with glory.

Whom have I in heaven but you?
And there is nothing upon earth that I desire
  in comparison with you.

Though my flesh and my heart fail me,
God is the strength of my heart and my portion for ever.

Psalm 73.23—26

May you be strengthened with all power, giving thanks to the Father who has qualified us to share in the inheritance of the saints in light. He has delivered us from the dominion of darkness and transferred us to the kingdom of his beloved Son, in whom we have redemption, the forgiveness of sins.

Colossians 1.11a, 12—14

Daily reading and reflection concludes with

The Word became flesh and dwelt among us,
full of grace and truth.

The Gospel Canticle: Magnificat

✠ My soul proclaims the greatness of the Lord,
   my spirit rejoices in God my Saviour;
he has looked with favour on his lowly servant.

From this day all generations will call me blessed;
the Almighty has done great things for me
   and holy is his name.

He has mercy on those who fear him,
from generation to generation.

He has shown strength with his arm
and has scattered the proud in their conceit,

Casting down the mighty from their thrones
and lifting up the lowly.

He has filled the hungry with good things
and sent the rich away empty.

He has come to the aid of his servant Israel,
to remember his promise of mercy,

The promise made to our ancestors,
to Abraham and his children for ever.

Luke 1.46–55

Glory to the Father and to the Son and to the Holy Spirit;
as it was in the beginning is now and shall be for ever. Amen.

Prayer

Each day of the week there is opportunity to reflect on a different aspect of what God in Christ is doing for us, and for the needs of the world.

On Sundays

For the ministry and mission of God's Church

Almighty God,
by triumphing over the powers of darkness
Christ has prepared a place for us in the new Jerusalem:
may we, who have this day given thanks for his resurrection,
praise him in the eternal city of which he is the light;
through Jesus Christ our Lord,
who is alive and reigns with you and the Holy Spirit,
one God, now and for ever.

On Mondays

That we may bring forth the fruits of the Spirit,
and for justice and peace for all

Almighty God,
who sent your Holy Spirit
to be the life and light of your Church:
open our hearts to the riches of your grace,
that we may bring forth the fruit of the Spirit
in love and joy and peace;
through Jesus Christ your Son our Lord,
who is alive and reigns with you,
in the unity of the Holy Spirit,
one God, now and for ever.

9th after Trinity

On Tuesdays

For the coming of God's kingdom,
for the leaders of the world and all in authority

Lord of all power and might,
the author and giver of all good things:
graft in our hearts the love of your name,
increase in us true religion,
nourish us with all goodness,
and of your great mercy keep us in the same;
through Jesus Christ your Son our Lord,
who is alive and reigns with you,
in the unity of the Holy Spirit,
one God, now and for ever.

7th after Trinity

On Wednesdays

For all who have not heard the Gospel,
and that we may recognize Christ's presence in our midst

Eternal God,
the light of the minds that know thee,
the joy of the hearts that love thee
and the strength of the wills that serve thee;
grant us so to know thee that we may truly love thee,
and so to love thee that we may fully serve thee,
whom to serve is perfect freedom,
in Jesus Christ our Lord.

After St Augustine

For the peace of the world and the unity of the Church,
and for the healing of relationships

Almighty and everlasting God,
by whose Spirit the whole body of the Church
is governed and sanctified:
hear our prayer which we offer for all your faithful people,
that in their vocation and ministry
they may serve you in holiness and truth
to the glory of your name;
through our Lord and Saviour Jesus Christ,
who is alive and reigns with you,
in the unity of the Holy Spirit,
one God, now and for ever.

5th after Trinity

On Fridays

For the sick and the suffering,
for the victims of our inhumanity
and for forgiveness and repentance for our wrongdoing

Most merciful God,
who by the death and resurrection of your Son Jesus Christ
delivered and saved the world:
grant that by faith in him who suffered on the cross
we may triumph in the power of his victory;
through Jesus Christ your Son our Lord,
who is alive and reigns with you,
in the unity of the Holy Spirit,
one God, now and for ever.

5th of Lent

On Saturdays

> For the departed, that they may have rest and peace,
> and for ourselves, that we may live as citizens of heaven

> Merciful God,
> you have prepared for those who love you
> such good things as pass our understanding:
> pour into our hearts such love toward you
> that we, loving you in all things and above all things,
> may obtain your promises,
> which exceed all that we can desire;
> through Jesus Christ your Son our Lord,
> who is alive and reigns with you,
> in the unity of the Holy Spirit,
> one God, now and for ever.

6th after Trinity

Daily, Evening Prayer concludes with the Lord's Prayer where we unite all our prayer in Christ's perpetual prayer to the Father.

> Our Father, who art in heaven,
> hallowed be thy name;
> thy kingdom come;
> thy will be done;
> on earth as it is in heaven.
> Give us this day our daily bread.
> And forgive us our trespasses,
> as we forgive those who trespass against us.
> And lead us not into temptation;
> but deliver us from evil.
> For thine is the kingdom,
> the power and the glory
> for ever and ever. Amen.

We unite ourselves with all for whom we pray, and commend ourselves to God's mercy for his blessing.

> The grace of our Lord Jesus Christ,
> and the love of God,
> and the fellowship of the Holy Spirit,
> be with us all evermore.
> Amen.

3.5 Night Prayer

May the Lord Almighty grant me a quiet night and a perfect end.
Amen.

Show us your mercy, O Lord,
and grant us your salvation.

Pause to recollect the sins and omissions of the day.

May Almighty God, have mercy upon me,
forgive me my sins, and bring me to everlasting life. Amen.

Glory to the Father and to the Son and to the Holy Spirit;
as it was in the beginning is now and shall be for ever. Amen.
Alleluia.

Some verses of the psalms traditionally said each night follow.

In peace I will lie down and sleep,
for it is you, Lord, only, who make me dwell safely.

Psalm 4.8

Whoever dwells in the shelter of the Most High
and abides under the shadow of the Almighty,
shall say to the Lord, 'My refuge and my stronghold,
my God, in whom I put my trust.'

He shall cover you with his wings
  and you shall be safe under his feathers;
his faithfulness and truth shall be your shield and buckler.

There shall no evil happen to you,
neither shall any plague come near your tent.

For he shall give his angels charge over you,
to keep you in all your ways.

They shall bear you in their hands,
lest you dash your foot against a stone.

Psalm 91.1,2,10—12

Come, bless the Lord, all you servants of the Lord,
you that by night stand in the house of the Lord.

Lift up your hands towards the sanctuary
and bless the Lord.

The Lord that made heaven and earth
give you blessing out of Zion.

Psalm 134

Glory to the Father and to the Son and to the Holy Spirit;
as it was in the beginning is now and shall be for ever. Amen.

One of the following short readings may be used.

You, O Lord, are in the midst of us and we are called by your name;
leave us not, O Lord our God.

Jeremiah 14.9

or

Be sober, be vigilant, because your adversary the devil is prowling
round like a roaring lion, seeking for someone to devour. Resist him,
strong in the faith.

1 Peter 5.8,9

or

You will keep them in perfect peace, whose minds are stayed on you,
because they trust in you.

Isaiah 26.3

or

Fear not, for I have redeemed you; I have called you by name, you are
mine.

Isaiah 43.1b

Reflection on the readings concludes with:

Into your hands, O Lord, I commend my spirit,
for you have redeemed me, Lord God of truth.

Keep me as the apple of your eye;
hide me under the shadow of your wings.

The Gospel Canticle: The Song of Simeon

Save us, O Lord, while waking
and guard us while sleeping,
that awake we may watch with Christ
and asleep we may rest in peace.

☩ Lord, now lettest thou thy servant depart in peace:
According to thy word.
For mine eyes have seen thy salvation
Which thou hast prepared before the face of all people.
To be a light to lighten the gentiles:
and to be the glory of your people Israel.

Glory to the Father and to the Son and to the Holy Spirit;
as it was in the beginning is now and shall be for ever. Amen.

Save us, O Lord, while waking
and guard us while sleeping,
that awake we may watch with Christ
and asleep we may rest in peace.

Prayer follows, concluding with one or more of these collects.

Visit this place, O Lord, we pray,
and drive far from it all the snares of the enemy;
may your holy angels dwell with us and guard us in peace,
and may your blessing be upon us evermore;
through Jesus Christ, our Lord. Amen

or

Lighten our darkness, Lord, we pray,
and in your great mercy
defend us from all perils and dangers of this night
for the love of your only Son,
our Saviour, Jesus Christ. Amen.

or

Look down, O God, from your heavenly throne,
illuminate the darkness of this night with your celestial brightness,
and from the children of light banish the deeds of darkness;
through Jesus Christ, our Lord. Amen.

Be present, O merciful God,
and protect us through the silent hours of this night,
so that we who are wearied
by the changes and chances of this fleeting world
may rest on your eternal changelessness;
through Jesus Christ, our Lord. Amen.

or

O Lord Jesus Christ, Son of the living God,
who at this evening hour didst rest in the sepulchre
and didst thereby sanctify the grave to be a bed of hope to thy people:
make us so to abound in sorrow for our sins,
which were the cause of thy passion,
that when our bodies lie in the dust,
our souls may live with thee;
who livest and reignest with the Father and the Holy Spirit,
one God, world without end. Amen.

In conclusion, Christaraksha – *an Indian prayer before sleep.*

May the cross of the Son of God,
which is mightier than all the hosts of Satan,
and more glorious than all the hosts of heaven,
abide with me in my going out and my coming in.
By day and night, at morning and at evening,
at all times and in all places
may it protect and defend me.
From the wrath of evildoers,
from the assaults of evil spirits,
from foes visible and invisible,
from the snares of the devil,
from all passions that beguile the soul and body
may it guard, protect and deliver me.

or

Salve Regina.

This anthem is traditionally sung at the end of Night Prayer.

> Salve, Regina, mater misericordiae;
> *Hail, O Queen, mother of mercy;*
>
> vita, dulcedo et spes nostra, salve.
> *our life, our sweetness and our hope, hail.*
>
> Ad te clamamus, exsules, filii Evae,
> *To you do we cry, the banished, children of Eve,*
>
> ad te suspiramus,
> *to you do we sigh,*
>
> gementes et flentes in hac lacrimarum valle;
> *lamenting and weeping in this vale of tears;*
>
> eia, ergo, advocata nostra,
> *therefore, our advocate,*
>
> illos tuos misericordes oculos ad nos converte,
> *your eyes of mercy turn towards us,*
>
> Et Iesum, benedictum fructum ventris tui,
> *And Jesus, the blessèd fruit of your womb,*
>
> nobis post hoc exsilium ostende,
> *to us, after this exile, reveal,*
>
> O clemens, O pia, O dulcis Virgo Maria.
> *O clement, O devoted, O sweet Virgin Mary.*

or

Armenian Orthodox Dismissal:

> Keep us in peace, O Christ our God,
> under the protection of your holy and venerable cross;
> save us from our enemies, visible and invisible,
> and count us worthy to glorify you with thanksgiving,
> with the Father and the Holy Spirit,
> now and for ever, world without end. Amen.

The Eucharist

4   The Eucharist

At the heart of the Church's worship is the Eucharist. In our baptism we are made one with Christ in his dying and rising, and it is this union with God in Christ that we affirm in the Eucharist. Baptism celebrates the start of our new life in Christ; sharing in the celebration of the Eucharist is how we grow.

There are many names for the Eucharist. The early disciples called it the Breaking of the Bread. In the Orthodox tradition it is simply called the Liturgy while in the West it is more commonly called the Mass, the Lord's Supper or Holy Communion. Each of these names stresses a different aspect of the offering of our lives. Eucharist means thanksgiving, Liturgy implies the offering of our worship, Mass comes from the Latin for dismissal — going out from worship to be what we have become — and Holy Communion stresses the personal union of each worshipper with God. All these names show ways in which the Church down the ages has tried to be faithful to Jesus' command to his disciples at the Last Supper: 'Do this in remembrance of me.'

Whatever the name, the Eucharist is at the heart of the Christian's life. Each of us has the responsibility to join others in celebrating each week — Sunday is a weekly reminder of Easter — and on every major commemoration and festival in the Church's annual year, what God in Christ has done for us.

The importance of this celebration is captured by Dom Gregory Dix in The Shape of the Liturgy:

> Jesus told his friends to do this, and they have done it always since. Was ever another command so obeyed? For century after century, spreading slowly to every continent and country and among every race on earth, this action has been done, in every conceivable human circumstance, for every conceivable human need, from infancy and before it, to extreme old age and beyond it; from the pinnacles of earthly greatness to the refuge of fugitives in the caves and dens of the earth. Men have found no better thing than this to do for kings at their crowning and for criminals going to the scaffold; for armies in triumph, or for a bride and bridegroom in a little country church; while the hiss of scythes in the thick June grass came faintly through the windows of the church; tremulously, by an old monk on the fiftieth anniversary of his

vows; furtively, by an exiled bishop, who has hewn timber all day in a prison camp near Murmansk; gorgeously, for the canonisation of St Joan of Arc – one could fill many pages with why men have done this, and not tell a hundredth part of them. And best of all, week by week and month by month, on a hundred thousand successive Sundays, faithfully, unfailingly, across all the parishes of Christendom, the pastors have done just this to make the 'plebs sancta Dei' – the holy common people of God.

In the celebration of the Eucharist, we recall what God has done for us in Christ: first he shares our life; then he changes it. So the twin peaks of each celebration are the proclaiming of the Gospel, where we celebrate the Word made flesh, dwelling in our midst, and the Breaking of the Bread, where we celebrate the presence of Christ's dying and rising in the broken bread we share.

You can see how the early Church united the practice of going to the Temple or Synagogue to hear the Word of God with returning to their homes to celebrate Christ's fulfilment of these promises in the Breaking of the Bread in the Acts of the Apostles:

And all who believed were together and had all things in common; … and day by day, attending the temple together and breaking bread in their homes, they partook of food with glad and generous hearts, praising God and having favour with all the people. And the Lord added to their number day by day those who were being saved. *Acts 2.43–47*

The shape of the Eucharist and its direct relationship to the disciples' experience of the transformation of their sense of loss and hopelessness at the death of Jesus is best understood by reading the account of the Journey to Emmaus in chapter 24 of Luke's Gospel. There the narrative falls into four main sections: verses 11–24, where the stranger who walks with the disciples gets them to tell him of their loss and disappointment; verses 25–27, where Jesus explains the references to the Messiah's suffering and death in the Old Testament by reference to himself; verses 28–31, where Jesus enters with them, takes the bread, blesses, breaks and gives it to them and their eyes are opened; and verses 32–35, where their encounter with the real presence of the living Christ spurs them into instant action. This four-fold shape has come to give the Eucharist its traditional form.

So the Shape for the Eucharist (Order One in Common Worship)
has four main sections:

§   The Gathering
during which we, the individual members of the body of Christ, are
drawn into being a congregation by singing together, by being recalled in
penitence to our baptismal status, and so are prepared to receive the Word
of God. This section is summed up in the Collect, said by the bishop or
priest who presides at the celebration.

§   The Liturgy of the Word
during which we engage with the Word, as the story of what God has
done in Christ is set alongside our experience, and in the Sermon the
implications are teased out for prayer in the Intercession and action
in our daily lives.

§   The Liturgy of the Sacrament
during which we are offered the possibility of transformation as we are
incorporated into the one, perfect self-offering of Christ to the Father
and receive the body and blood of Christ by faith with thanksgiving.

§   The Dismissal
when we are reminded to put into practice the new life we have received,
and are sent out into the community to do it.

4.1   Preparing to Celebrate the Eucharist

Preparation for the celebration traditionally includes one or more of these three forms: reviewing your spiritual health by an act of recollection and penitence, making a formal Confession; preparing the Sunday readings, especially meditating on the Gospel; and, third, using a traditional pattern of Prayers of Preparation, such as became formalized for the clergy as they vested and went to the altar at the start of the celebration.

In any case, these prayers may be used:

For reflection

O taste and see how gracious the Lord is.
Blessed are those who trust in him.

On a Saturday night

As the nightwatch looks for the morning,
so do we look for you, O Christ.
Come with the dawning of the day,
and make yourself known to us
in the breaking of bread.
For you are our God, for ever and ever.

Making a Formal Confession

Whether or not you make a formal Confession, you may find the prayers and readings in Chapter 6, Sin and its Remedy (p.199) helpful in reviewing the state of your spiritual health. It is a well-established custom to make a formal Confession at least before the major festivals of the Church's year, at Christmas and Easter.

You may choose instead to use the Beatitudes or the Summary of the Law as a way of reflecting on the week that has passed, and some of the prayers in Chapter 6 (p.201)

Blessèd are the poor in spirit,
for theirs is the kingdom of heaven.

Blessèd are those who mourn,
for they shall be comforted.

Blessèd are the meek,
for they shall inherit the earth.

Blessèd are those who hunger and thirst after righteousness,
for they shall be satisfied.

Blessèd are the merciful,
for they shall obtain mercy.

Blessèd are the pure in heart,
for they shall see God.

Blessèd are the peacemakers,
for they shall be called children of God.

Blessèd are those who suffer persecution for righteousness' sake,
for theirs is the kingdom of heaven.

Matthew 5.3–10

Our Lord's Summary of the Law:

Hear, O Israel, the Lord our God is the only God,
and you shall love him with all your heart, and soul and mind.
The second command is like, namely this:
You shall love your neighbour as yourself.
There is no other command greater than these;
On these two commandments hang all the law and the prophets.

Preparing the Sunday Gospel

*One way of preparing for the Eucharist the night before is to read the Gospel for the
following day. Before you read the passage, you may recall:*

It is the God who said, 'Let light shine out of darkness,' who has
shone in our hearts to give the light of the knowledge of the glory
of God in the face of Jesus Christ.

2 Corinthians 4.6

Your word is a lantern to my feet and a light upon our path.

Psalm 119.105

*Then read the Gospel of the Day, imagining that you are there and that Jesus'
words are addressed to you directly.*

Here are words you can trust:
Remember Jesus Christ, risen from the dead.
He is our salvation, our eternal glory.
If we have died with him, we shall also live with him;
if we endure, we shall also reign with him.
If we are faithless, he keeps faith;
for he has broken the power of death
and brought life and immortality to light through the gospel.

You may use this prayer, or the Collect of the following day:

Blessed Lord,
who caused all holy Scriptures to be written for our learning:
help us so to hear them,
to read, mark, learn and inwardly digest them
that, through patience, and the comfort of your holy word,
we may embrace and for ever hold fast
the hope of everlasting life,
which you have given us in our Saviour Jesus Christ,
who is alive and reigns with you,
in the unity of the Holy Spirit,
one God, now and for ever.

The Conclusion:

Let us bless the living God:

He was born of the Virgin Mary,
revealed in his glory,
worshipped by angels,
proclaimed among the nations,
believed in throughout the world,
exalted to the highest heavens.

Blessèd be God, our strength and our salvation,
now and for ever. Amen.

The Rite of Preparation

These are among the prayers the clergy prayed in the medieval Sarum rite as they vested, and as they approached the altar.

Come, Holy Ghost, our souls inspire,
And lighten with celestial fire;
Thou the anointing Spirit art,
Who dost thy sevenfold gifts impart:

Thy blessèd unction from above
Is comfort, life, and fire of love;
Enable with perpetual light
The dullness of our blinded sight:

Anoint and cheer our soilèd face
With the abundance of thy grace:
Keep far our foes, give peace at home;
Where thou art guide no ill can come.

Teach us to know the Father, Son,
And thee, of both, to be but One;
That through the ages all along
This may be our endless song,

Praise to thy eternal merit,
Father, Son, and Holy Spirit. Amen.

John Cosin (1594-1672)

I will go unto the altar of God,
the God of my joy and gladness.

Give judgement for me, O God,
and defend my cause against an ungodly people;
deliver me from the deceitful and the wicked.

For you are the God of my refuge;
why have you cast me from you,
and why go I so heavily, while the enemy oppresses me?

O send out your light and your truth, that they may lead me,
and bring me to your holy hill and to your dwelling,

That I may go to the altar of God,
to the God of my joy and gladness;
and on the lyre I will give thanks to you, O God my God.

Why are you so full of heaviness, O my soul,
and why are you so disquieted within me?

O put your trust in God;
for I will yet give him thanks,
who is the help of my countenance, and my God.

I will go unto the altar of God,
the God of my joy and gladness.

From Psalm 43

Our help is in the name of the Lord;
the maker of heaven and earth.

Cleanse our consciences, Lord, we pray;
that when our Lord Jesus Christ comes
he may find in us a mansion prepared for himself;
who with you and the Holy Spirit lives and reigns,
one God, for ever and ever.

Gelasian Sacramentary

The Collect for Purity:

Almighty God,
to whom all hearts are open,
all desires known
and from whom no secrets are hidden:
cleanse the thoughts of our hearts
by the inspiration of your Holy Spirit,
that we may perfectly love you,
and worthily magnify your holy name;
through Christ our Lord. Amen.

4.2   The Order of the Eucharist

As you enter the church, remember your baptism and make the sign of the cross,
using the holy water from the basin by the door if that is provided, or else from the font,
saying:

⛨ In the name of the Father,
and of the Son,
and of the Holy Spirit. Amen

When you have found a place, look round and remember those for whom you specially
want to pray whether present or not. Thank God for the opportunity to worship freely
and remember those who cannot be at the Eucharist, through sickness or because a job
prevents them being there or because there is no priest where they live. You may like to
remember the notice displayed in many churches:

> Before the Eucharist – speak to God
> During the Eucharist – let God speak to you
> After the Eucharist – speak to one another

The Gathering

At the entrance

As the ministers enter, the assembly rises. This is not because the people – whether
choir or servers or clergy – are important, but because the Deacon brings in the
Gospel Book, holding it up as a sign that the living Word of God, Christ himself,
is coming among his people. The Gospel Book sometimes has a richly decorated
cover, with an icon of Christ embossed on it.

The assembly is gathered by the presiding celebrant's Greeting, and the task of
collecting the scattered fragments of our human endeavour into a united offering of
praise and thanksgiving begins.

Order One

¶ *The Gathering*

At the entry of the ministers a hymn may be sung.

The president may say

In the name of the Father,
and of the Son,
and of the Holy Spirit.

All　**Amen.**

The Greeting

The president greets the people

The Lord be with you
All　**and also with you.**

(or)

Grace, mercy and peace
from God our Father
and the Lord Jesus Christ
be with you
All　**and also with you.**

From Easter Day to Pentecost this acclamation follows

Alleluia. Christ is risen.
All　**He is risen indeed. Alleluia.**

Words of welcome or introduction may be said.

At the Confession

As we tell the story of who we are before God, we recall our sins and make a Confession. This may take various forms:

> * *A prayer of confession, said together and introduced by a bidding*

> * *Verses from the psalms, or other scripture, to introduce the Kyrie eleison*

> * *A Blessing of the Water, followed by sprinkling of the assembly as a reminder of baptism (specially in Eastertide)*

When the Lord comes, he will bring to light things now hidden in darkness, and will disclose the purposes of the heart.

> Not unto us, O Lord, not unto us, but unto thy name give the praise.
>   Kyrie eleison
> Wash me, O Lord, and I shall be whiter than snow.
>   Christe eleison
> Make me a clean heart, O God, and renew a right Spirit within me.
>   Kyrie eleison

In the tender compassion of our God, the dawn from on high shall break upon us, to shine on those who dwell in darkness and the shadow of death, and to guide our feet into the way of peace.

Prayers of Penitence

The Commandments, the Beatitudes, the Comfortable Words or the Summary of the Law may be used

All **Almighty God, our heavenly Father,**
we have sinned against you
and against our neighbour
in thought and word and deed,
through negligence, through weakness,
through our own deliberate fault.
We are truly sorry
and repent of all our sins.
For the sake of your Son Jesus Christ,
who died for us,
forgive us all that is past
and grant that we may serve you in newness of life
to the glory of your name.
Amen.

(or)

All **Most merciful God,**
Father of our Lord Jesus Christ,
we confess that we have sinned
in thought, word and deed.
We have not loved you with our whole heart.
We have not loved our neighbours as ourselves.
In your mercy
forgive what we have been,
help us to amend what we are,
and direct what we shall be;
that we may do justly,
love mercy,
and walk humbly with you, our God.
Amen.

Or, with suitable penitential sentences, the Kyrie eleison may be used

Lord, have mercy.
All **Lord, have mercy.**
Christ, have mercy.
All **Christ, have mercy.**
Lord, have mercy.
All **Lord, have mercy.**

At the Gloria

For the TRUMPET OF God is a blessed intelligence and so
  are all the instruments in HEAVEN.
For GOD the father Almighty plays upon the HARP of
  stupendous magnitude and melody.
For innumerable Angels fly out at every touch and
  his tune is a work of creation.
For at that time malignity ceases and the devils
  themselves are at peace.
For this time is perceptible to man by a remarkable
  stillness and serenity of soul.

From Jubilate Agno by Christopher Smart (1722-1771)

At the Collect

The president calls for a moment of silent prayer, and then offers the assembly and its needs
to God, conscious of his gifts and his mercy, and praying that he will graciously
hear us. This prayer concludes the Gathering, and the assembly sits.

Almighty God,
who forgives all who truly repent,
have mercy upon *you*,
pardon and deliver *you* from all *your* sins,
confirm and strengthen *you* in all goodness,
and keep *you* in life eternal;
through Jesus Christ our Lord.

All **Amen.**

Gloria in Excelsis

The Gloria in Excelsis may be used

All **Glory to God in the highest,**
and peace to his people on earth.
Lord God, heavenly King,
almighty God and Father,
we worship you, we give you thanks,
we praise you for your glory.
Lord Jesus Christ, only Son of the Father,
Lord God, Lamb of God,
you take away the sin of the world:
have mercy on us;
you are seated at the right hand of the Father:
receive our prayer.
For you alone are the Holy One,
you alone are the Lord,
you alone are the Most High, Jesus Christ,
with the Holy Spirit,
in the glory of God the Father.
Amen.

The Collect

The president introduces a period of silent prayer with the words
'Let us pray' or a more specific bidding.

The Collect is said, and all respond

All **Amen.**

The Liturgy of the Word

In the Liturgy of the Word, the gathered Church with its unconscious as well as expressed needs is confronted by the story of what God has done for his people. The readings are not those we have chosen because we like them or find them comforting. They are part of a set pattern that the Churches throughout the world are reading that day, and so the Church is confronted by what God says. There may be readings from both the Old Testament and the New, but there is always the proclamation of the Gospel. There God in Christ speaks to us directly, face to face, and we stand to greet him with Alleluias. Do we expect a living encounter?

> Cor ad cor loquitur
> *Heart speaks to heart*

Cardinal Newman's motto

> Where lies your landmark, seamark, or soul's star?
> There's none but truth can stead you. Christ is truth.

Gerard Manley Hopkins (1844-1889)

At the Alleluias

> Thousands of thousands stand around
> thy throne, O God most high;
> ten thousand times ten thousand sound
> thy praise; but who am I?
>
> Thy brightness unto them appears,
> whilst I thy footsteps trace;
> a sound of God comes to my ears,
> but they behold thy face:
> They sing, because thou art their sun.
> Lord, send a beam on me;
> For where heaven is but once begun,
> There alleluias be.

John Mason (c.1645-1694)

At the Gospel

At the Proclamation of the Gospel, the Deacon carries the Book of the Gospels into the middle of the assembly as a sign of Christ's coming among us.

> The Word was made flesh, and dwelt among us,
> full of grace and truth.

Readings

Either one or two readings from scripture precede the Gospel reading.

At the end of each the reader may say

This is the word of the Lord.

All **Thanks be to God.**

The psalm or canticle follows the first reading; other hymns and songs may be used between the readings.

Gospel Reading

This acclamation or another may herald the Gospel reading.

Alleluia, alleluia.

Speak, Lord, for your servant is listening.
You have the words of eternal life.   *1 Samuel 3.9; John 6.68*

All **Alleluia.**

When the Gospel is announced the reader says

The Lord be with you

All **and also with you.**

Hear the Gospel of our Lord Jesus Christ according to *N.*

All **Glory to you, O Lord.**

At the end

This is the Gospel of the Lord.

All **Praise to you, O Christ.**

Sermon

At the Creed

The Creeds of the Church are the formal professions of faith, and although the Apostles' Creed has always been part of the rite of Baptism, the Nicene Creed only became a part of the Eucharist relatively late. Much of what we believe about the nature of God's acts in creation, redemption and our sanctification is rehearsed in the Eucharistic Prayer, so the Creed is not always said.

What we are doing in saying the Creed is identifying ourselves with what the Church has always believed. The Creed is known in Greek and Latin as the Symbol; it is more like a historic flag or coat of arms to which we pledge our allegiance than a detailed photograph of all we believe.

The Church is Catholic, universal, so are all her actions; all that she does belongs to all. When she baptizes a child, that action concerns me; for that child is thereby connected to that Head which is my Head too, and engrafted into that body, whereof I am a member. And when she buries a man, that action concerns me. No man is an island entire of itself; every man is a piece of the continent. Any man's death diminishes me, because I am involved in mankind; and therefore never send to know for whom the bell tolls; it tolls for thee.

John Donne (1573-1631)

I bind unto myself the name,
The strong name of the Trinity;
By invocation of the same,
The Three in One, and One in Three.
Of whom all nature hath creation;
Eternal Father, Spirit, Word:
Praise to the Lord of my salvation,
Salvation is of Christ the Lord.

From St Patrick's Breastplate

The Creed

On Sundays and Principal Holy Days an authorized translation of the Nicene Creed is used, or on occasion the Apostles' Creed or an authorized Affirmation of Faith may be used.

All   **We believe in one God,
the Father, the Almighty,
maker of heaven and earth,
of all that is,
seen and unseen.**

**We believe in one Lord, Jesus Christ,
the only Son of God,
eternally begotten of the Father,
God from God, Light from Light,
true God from true God,
begotten, not made,
of one Being with the Father;
through him all things were made.
For us and for our salvation he came down from heaven,
was incarnate from the Holy Spirit and the Virgin Mary
and was made man.
For our sake he was crucified under Pontius Pilate;
he suffered death and was buried.
On the third day he rose again
in accordance with the Scriptures;
he ascended into heaven
and is seated at the right hand of the Father.
He will come again in glory to judge the living and the dead,
and his kingdom will have no end.**

**We believe in the Holy Spirit,
the Lord, the giver of life,
who proceeds from the Father and the Son,
who with the Father and the Son is worshipped and glorified,
who has spoken through the prophets.
We believe in one holy catholic and apostolic Church.
We acknowledge one baptism for the forgiveness of sins.
We look for the resurrection of the dead,
and the life of the world to come.
Amen.**

To intercede means literally not to make petitions or indeed to
utter words at all but to meet, to encounter, to be with someone on
behalf of or in relation to others. Jesus is with the Father; with
him is the intimate response of perfect humanity; with him is the
power of Calvary and Easter; with him as one who bears us all
on his heart, our Son of Man, our friend, our priest; with him as
our own. That is the continuing intercession of Jesus the high
priest.

Michael Ramsey (1904-1988)

And though the last lights off the black West went
    Oh, morning, at the brown brink eastward, springs —
Because the Holy Ghost over the bent
    World broods with warm breast and with ah! bright wings.
Gerard Manley Hopkins (1844-1889)

Look graciously upon us, Holy Spirit,
and give us for our hallowing
thoughts that pass into prayer,
prayers that pass into love,
and love that passes into life with you for ever.

Almighty God, who hast given us grace at this time with one
accord to make our common supplications unto thee; and dost
promise, that when two or three are gathered together in thy
Name thou wilt grant their requests: Fulfil now, O Lord, the
desires and petitions of thy servants, as may be most expedient
for them; granting us in this world knowledge of thy truth,
and in the world to come life everlasting.

St John Chrysostom (349-407)
The Book of Common Prayer

Prayers of Intercession

The prayers usually include these concerns and may follow this sequence:

¶   *The Church of Christ*

¶   *Creation, human society, the Sovereign and those in authority*

¶   *The local community*

¶   *Those who suffer*

¶   *The communion of saints*

These responses may be used

Lord, in your mercy
All   **hear our prayer.**

(or)

Lord, hear us.
All   **Lord, graciously hear us.**

And at the end

Merciful Father,
All   **accept these prayers
for the sake of your Son,
our Saviour Jesus Christ.
Amen.**

or another suitable prayer

The Liturgy of the Sacrament

At the Peace

It is our union — each one of us — with God in Christ that draws us into him corporately and unites us with one another. We do not create it: it is his gift.

Greet one another with the kiss of peace

2 Corinthians (13.12)

In the Ambrosian rite in Milan, the deacon says at this point

As the Lord has taught us,
before presenting our gifts at the altar
let us be reconciled with the kiss of peace.

The Peace

*The president may introduce the Peace with a suitable sentence,
and then says*

The peace of the Lord be always with you
All **and also with you.**

These words may be added

Let us offer one another a sign of peace.

All may exchange a sign of peace.

At the Offering of the People

As the gifts are prepared at the altar, we recall that they represent us, all that we are and all that we bring, as we offer ourselves to God for his service.

> That poor widow, the church, casts in all her life into the treasury of God.
>
> *Irenaeus of Lyons (c.130-c.202)*

> It is the mystery of yourselves that is laid on the table of the Lord; that mystery you receive. To that which you are, you answer 'Amen', and in answering you assent. For you hear the words 'the Body of Christ' and you answer 'Amen'. Be a member of the Body of Christ that the Amen may be true.
>
> *St Augustine (354-430)*

> As this grain once scattered on the mountains was gathered together and made one bread, so, Lord, let your Church be gathered from the ends of the earth into your Kingdom.
>
> *From the Didache*

As water is mixed with wine in the chalice:

> By the mystery of this water and this wine,
> may he who shared our earthly life
> make us partakers of his divine nature.

Preparation of the Table
Taking of the Bread and Wine

A hymn may be sung.

The gifts of the people may be gathered and presented.

The table is prepared and bread and wine are placed upon it.

One or more of the prayers at the preparation of the table may be said.

Blessed are you, Lord God of all creation:
through your goodness we have this bread to set before you,
which earth has given and human hands have made.
It will become for us the bread of life.

All　**Blessed be God for ever.**

Blessed are you, Lord God of all creation:
through your goodness we have this wine to set before you,
fruit of the vine and work of human hands.
It will become for us the cup of salvation.

All　**Blessed be God for ever.**

(or)

Blessed be God,
by whose grace creation is renewed,
by whose love heaven is opened,
by whose mercy we offer our sacrifice of praise.

All　**Blessed be God for ever.**

(or)

Look upon us in mercy not in judgement;
draw us from hatred to love;
make the frailty of our praise
a dwelling place for your glory.

All　**Amen.**

(or)

Pour upon the poverty of our love,
and the weakness of our praise,
the transforming fire of your presence.

All　**Amen.**

The president takes the bread and wine

The Eucharistic Prayer

At the heart of the Eucharist is the great Prayer of Thanksgiving. There are a number of forms, but there are elements that are common to them all. The prayer always begins with an opening dialogue, *to bind the praying of the bishop or priest who presides over the assembly with the prayer of the whole worshipping community together. Culminating in the* Sanctus and Benedictus, *the presiding celebrant praises God for his mighty acts, and may include a particular thanksgiving (a* Proper Preface*) for what the Church celebrates that day, whether a season or a saint. After the Sanctus, the prayer focuses on what God has done in Christ, recalling the institution of the Eucharist at the Last Supper. Making the memorial of God's mighty acts in Christ (the* anamnesis*) may be endorsed by the assembly's* Acclamation, *and the prayer will include a petition for the coming of the Holy Spirit (the* epiclesis*), that the gifts of bread and wine may be the Body and Blood of Christ, and that those who receive them may be made one with Christ, and all who are in him, in this world and at the eternal banquet of heaven. The prayer ends with a* doxology of praise, *and a great Amen.*

At the Sanctus

> 'What, it will be questioned, when the Sun rises, do you not see a round disc of fire somewhat like a guinea?' 'Oh no, no, I see an innumerable company of the heavenly host crying, "Holy, Holy, Holy is the Lord God Almighty!"'
>
> *William Blake (1757-1827)*

The Eucharistic Prayer

The president says

The Lord be with you
All **and also with you.**

Lift up your hearts.
All **We lift them to the Lord.**

Let us give thanks to the Lord our God.
All **It is right to give thanks and praise.**

The president praises God for his mighty acts in these or other words (Prayer B)

Father, we give you thanks and praise
through your beloved Son Jesus Christ, your living Word,
through whom you have created all things;
who was sent by you in your great goodness to be our Saviour.
By the power of the Holy Spirit he took flesh;
as your Son, born of the blessed Virgin,
he lived on earth and went about among us;
he opened wide his arms for us on the cross;
he put an end to death by dying for us;
and revealed the resurrection by rising to new life;
so he fulfilled your will and won for you a holy people.

Short Proper Preface, when appropriate

Therefore with angels and archangels,
and with all the company of heaven,
we proclaim your great and glorious name,
for ever praising you and *saying*:

All **Holy, holy, holy Lord,**
God of power and might,
heaven and earth are full of your glory.
Hosanna in the highest.
[Blessed is he who comes in the name of the Lord.
Hosanna in the highest.]

Let all mortal flesh keep silence, and with fear and trembling stand;
Ponder nothing earthly minded, for with blessing in his hand
Christ our God to earth descendeth, our full homage to demand.

King of kings, yet born of Mary, as of old on earth he stood,
Lord of lords, in human vesture – in the Body and the Blood –
He will give to all the faithful his own Self for heavenly food.

Rank on rank the host of heaven spreads its vanguard on the way,
As the light of light descendeth from the realms of endless day,
That the powers of hell may vanish as the darkness clears away.

At his feet the six-winged seraph; Cherubim with sleepless eye
Veil their faces to the Presence, as with ceaseless voice they cry,
Alleluya, Alleluya, Alleluya, Lord most high.

From the Liturgy of St James, tr. G. Moultrie

Lord, you are holy indeed, the source of all holiness;
grant that by the power of your Holy Spirit,
and according to your holy will,
these gifts of bread and wine
may be to us the body and blood of our Lord Jesus Christ;
who, in the same night that he was betrayed,
took bread and gave you thanks;
he broke it and gave it to his disciples, saying:
Take, eat; this is my body which is given for you;
do this in remembrance of me.

In the same way, after supper
he took the cup and gave you thanks;
he gave it to them, saying:
Drink this, all of you;
this is my blood of the new covenant,
which is shed for you and for many for the forgiveness of sins.
Do this, as often as you drink it,
in remembrance of me.

One of these four acclamations may be used

[Great is the mystery of faith:]

All **Christ has died:**
Christ is risen:
Christ will come again.

(or)

[Praise to you, Lord Jesus:]

All **Dying you destroyed our death,**
rising you restored our life:
Lord Jesus, come in glory.

(or)

[Christ is the bread of life:]

All **When we eat this bread and drink this cup,**
we proclaim your death, Lord Jesus,
until you come in glory.

(or)

[Jesus Christ is Lord:]

All **Lord, by your cross and resurrection**
you have set us free.
You are the Saviour of the world.

At the end of the Eucharistic Prayer

Victim Divine, thy grace we claim
While thus thy precious death we show;
Once offered up, a spotless Lamb,
In thy great temple here below,
Thou didst for all mankind atone,
And standest now before the throne.

Thou standest in the holiest place,
As now for guilty sinners slain;
Thy blood of sprinkling speaks and prays
All-prevalent for helpless man;
Thy blood is still our ransom found,
And spreads salvation all around.

We need not now go up to heaven
To bring the long-sought Saviour down;
Thou art to all already given,
Thou dost e'en now thy banquet crown:
To every faithful soul appear,
And show thy real presence here.

Charles Wesley (1707-1788)

The prayer continues and leads into the doxology

And so, Father, calling to mind his death on the cross,
his perfect sacrifice made once for the sins of the whole world;
rejoicing in his mighty resurrection and glorious ascension,
and looking for his coming in glory,
we celebrate this memorial of our redemption.

As we offer you this our sacrifice of praise and thanksgiving,
we bring before you this bread and this cup
and we thank you for counting us worthy
to stand in your presence and serve you.

Send the Holy Spirit on your people
and gather into one in your kingdom
all who share this one bread and one cup,
so that we, in the company of [N *and*] all the saints,
may praise and glorify you for ever,
through Jesus Christ our Lord;
by whom, and with whom, and in whom,
in the unity of the Holy Spirit,
all honour and glory be yours, almighty Father,
for ever and ever.

All   **Amen.**

Prayers A and G end

All   **Blessing and honour and glory and power**
be yours for ever and ever.
Amen.

Receive therefore and eat the Body of Christ,
you who are already made members of Christ
within the body of Christ.

Take and drink the Blood of Christ:
lest you should fall apart,
drink that which binds you together;
lest you should feel cheap to yourselves,
drink that which bought you.
As this, when you eat and drink it, is changed into you,
so you are changed into the Body of Christ
by an obedient and holy life.

You are receiving (unless you receive unworthily)
that which you have begun to be.
Make sure, therefore, that you do not eat and drink
judgement to yourselves.
The one who receives the mystery of unity
and does not preserve the bond of peace
receives the mystery not for, but against, themselves.

St Augustine (354-430)

The Lord's Prayer

As our Saviour taught us, so we pray

All   **Our Father in heaven,**
hallowed be your name,
your kingdom come,
your will be done,
on earth as in heaven.
Give us today our daily bread.
Forgive us our sins
as we forgive those who sin against us.
Lead us not into temptation
but deliver us from evil.
For the kingdom, the power,
and the glory are yours
now and for ever.
Amen.

(or)

Let us pray with confidence as our Saviour has taught us

All   **Our Father, who art in heaven,**
hallowed be thy name;
thy kingdom come;
thy will be done;
on earth as it is in heaven.
Give us this day our daily bread.
And forgive us our trespasses,
as we forgive those who trespass against us.
And lead us not into temptation;
but deliver us from evil.
For thine is the kingdom,
the power and the glory,
for ever and ever.
Amen.

At the Breaking of the Bread

The bread must be broken if it is to be shared. But the moment of breaking recalls the breaking of that body on the cross, that Christ died that we might have life. Our life, our oneness with him and one another is only achieved at the cost of his death.

Unless a grain of wheat falls on the earth and dies, it remains alone; but if it dies, it bears a rich harvest.

John 12.24

'Twas God the word that spake it,
He took the bread and brake it;
And what the word did make it,
That I believe, and take it.

Queen Elizabeth I (1533-1603)

Welcome sweet and sacred cheer,
Welcome deare;
With me, in me, live and dwell:
For thy neatnesse passeth sight,
Thy delight
Passeth tongue or taste to tell.

Onely God, who gives perfumes,
flesh assumes,
And with it perfumes my heart.

Yet as Pomanders and wood
Still are good,
Yet being bruised are better sented:
God, to show how farre his love
Could improve,
Here, as broken, is presented.

From 'The Banquet', George Herbert (1593-1633)

Breaking of the Bread

The president breaks the consecrated bread.

We break this bread
to share in the body of Christ.

All **Though we are many, we are one body,
because we all share in one bread.**

(or)

Every time we eat this bread
and drink this cup,

All **we proclaim the Lord's death
until he comes.**

The Agnus Dei may be used as the bread is broken

All **Lamb of God,
you take away the sin of the world,
have mercy on us.**

**Lamb of God,
you take away the sin of the world,
have mercy on us.**

**Lamb of God,
you take away the sin of the world,
grant us peace.**

(or)

All **Jesus, Lamb of God,
have mercy on us.**

**Jesus, bearer of our sins,
have mercy on us.**

**Jesus, redeemer of the world,
grant us peace.**

Love

Love bade me welcome: yet my soul drew back,
    Guiltie of dust and sinne.
But quick-ey'd Love, observing me grow slack
    From my first entrance in,
Drew nearer to me, sweetly questioning,
    If I lack'd any thing.

A guest, I answer'd, worthy to be here:
    Love said, you shall be he.
I the unkinde, ungratefull? Ah my deare,
    I cannot look on thee.
Love took my hand, and smiling did reply,
    Who made the eyes but I?

Truth Lord, but I have marr'd them: let my shame
    Go where it doth deserve.
And know you not, sayes Love, who bore the blame?
    My deare, then I will serve.
You must sit down, sayes Love, and taste my meat:
    So I did sit and eat.

George Herbert (1593-1633)

Giving of Communion

The president says one of these invitations to communion

Draw near with faith.
Receive the body of our Lord Jesus Christ
which he gave for you,
and his blood which he shed for you.
Eat and drink
in remembrance that he died for you,
and feed on him in your hearts
by faith with thanksgiving.

(or)

Jesus is the Lamb of God
who takes away the sin of the world.
Blessed are those who are called to his supper.

All **Lord, I am not worthy to receive you,
but only say the word, and I shall be healed.**

(or)

God's holy gifts
for God's holy people.

All **Jesus Christ is holy,
Jesus Christ is Lord,
to the glory of God the Father.**

or, from Easter Day to Pentecost

Alleluia. Christ our passover is sacrificed for us.

All **Therefore let us keep the feast. Alleluia.**

During the distribution of Communion

> Lord Jesus Christ, Son of the living God,
> whose death restored life to the world;
> deliver me from all my sins and from every evil
> through your most sacred Body and Blood,
> keep me ever in the ways of your commandments,
> and suffer me never to be separated from you.

From the Roman Liturgy, 9th century

The Call

Come, my Way, my Truth, my Life:
Such a Way, as gives us breath:
Such a Truth, as ends all strife:
Such a Life, as killeth death.

Come, my Light, my Feast, my Strength:
Such a Light, as shows a feast:
Such a Feast, as mends in length:
Such a Strength, as makes his guest.

Come, my Joy, my Love, my Heart:
Such a Joy, as none can move:
Such a Love, as none can part:
Such a Heart, as joys in love.

George Herbert (1593-1633)

Anima Christi

Soul of Christ, sanctify me.
Body of Christ, save me.
Blood of Christ, inebriate me.
Water from the side of Christ, wash me.
Passion of Christ, strengthen me.
Within thy wounds hide me.
Suffer me not to be separated from thee.
From the malicious enemy defend me.
In the hour of my death call me,
And bid me come to thee,
That with thy saints I may praise thee
For ever and ever. Amen

All **We do not presume**
to come to this your table, merciful Lord,
trusting in our own righteousness,
but in your manifold and great mercies.
We are not worthy
so much as to gather up the crumbs under your table.
But you are the same Lord
whose nature is always to have mercy.
Grant us therefore, gracious Lord,
so to eat the flesh of your dear Son Jesus Christ
and to drink his blood,
that our sinful bodies may be made clean by his body
and our souls washed through his most precious blood,
and that we may evermore dwell in him, and he in us.
Amen.

(or)

All **Most merciful Lord,**
your love compels us to come in.
Our hands were unclean,
our hearts were unprepared;
we were not fit
even to eat the crumbs from under your table.
But you, Lord, are the God of our salvation,
and share your bread with sinners.
So cleanse and feed us
with the precious body and blood of your Son,
that he may live in us and we in him;
and that we, with the whole company of Christ,
may sit and eat in your kingdom.
Amen.

The president and people receive communion.

Authorized words of distribution are used and the communicant replies

Amen.

During the distribution hymns and anthems may be sung.

After Communion

Finished and perfected, O Christ our Lord, so far as in us lies,
is the mystery of our redemption.
We have made the memorial of your death,
we have seen the figure of your resurrection,
we have been filled with your unending life.
We have tasted your inexhaustible goodness,
of which we pray you to count us worthy
both now and in the world to come.

The Liturgy of St Basil

Fill us, good Lord, with your Spirit of love;
and as you have fed us with the one bread of heaven,
so make us one in heart and mind;
through Jesus Christ our Lord.

Westcott House

We thank you, Lord,
that you have fed us in this holy sacrament,
united us with Christ,
and given us a foretaste of the heavenly banquet
prepared for all your people.

The Methodist Book of Worship

Prayer after Communion

Silence is kept.

The Post Communion or another suitable prayer is said.

All may say one of these prayers

All **Almighty God,
we thank you for feeding us
with the body and blood of your Son Jesus Christ.
Through him we offer you our souls and bodies
to be a living sacrifice.
Send us out
in the power of your Spirit
to live and work
to your praise and glory.
Amen.**

(or)

All **Father of all,
we give you thanks and praise,
that when we were still far off
you met us in your Son and brought us home.
Dying and living, he declared your love,
gave us grace, and opened the gate of glory.
May we who share Christ's body live his risen life;
we who drink his cup bring life to others;
we whom the Spirit lights give light to the world.
Keep us firm in the hope you have set before us,
so we and all your children shall be free,
and the whole earth live to praise your name;
through Christ our Lord.
Amen.**

The Sending Out

At the end of the Eucharist, we cannot ignore what we have become – members of Christ's body, alive with his life and ready to live it. But if his life is to flood the world with God's grace, then we have to take responsibility for it. The end of each Eucharist is a renewal of the day of Pentecost, when the disciples, their hearts on fire, were driven by the Spirit to put their faith into practice.

At the Dismissal

> Strengthen for Service, Lord, the hands which have been
> held out to receive the holy things;
> Grant that the ears which have heard the music of thy songs
> may be closed to clamour and dispute;
> That the eyes which have seen thy great love
> may also behold thy blessed hope;
> That the tongues which have sung Holy, Holy
> may also speak the truth;
> That the feet that have trodden thy courts
> may ever walk in the paths of light;
> That the bodies which have tasted thy living Body
> may be restored to newness of life.

The Liturgy of Malabar

> You are Christians! Then your Lord is one and the same
> with Jesus on his throne of glory,
> with Jesus in his Blessed Sacrament,
> with Jesus who is mystically with you as you pray,
> and with Jesus enshrined in the hearts and bodies of his brothers
> and sisters up and down the world.

> Now go out into the highways and hedges, and look for Jesus
> in the ragged and the naked,
> in the oppressed and the sweated,
> in those who have lost hope,
> and in those who are struggling to make good.
> Look for Jesus in them; and when you find him,
> gird yourselves with the towel of fellowship,
> and wash his feet in the person of his brethren.

Bishop Frank Weston (1871-1924)

¶   *The Dismissal*

A hymn may be sung.

The president may use the seasonal blessing, or another suitable blessing

(or)

The peace of God,
which passes all understanding,
keep your hearts and minds
in the knowledge and love of God,
and of his Son Jesus Christ our Lord;
and the blessing of God almighty,
the Father, the Son, and the Holy Spirit,
be among you and remain with you always.

All   **Amen.**

A minister says

Go in peace to love and serve the Lord.

All   **In the name of Christ. Amen.**

(or)

Go in the peace of Christ.

All   **Thanks be to God.**

or, from Easter Day to Pentecost

Go in the peace of Christ. Alleluia, alleluia.

All   **Thanks be to God. Alleluia, alleluia.**

The ministers and people depart.

After the Eucharist

Almighty and everliving God, we most heartily thank thee, for that thou dost vouchsafe to feed us, who have duly received these holy mysteries, with the spiritual food of the most precious Body and Blood of thy Son our Saviour Jesus Christ; and dost assure us thereby of thy favour and goodness towards us; and that we are very members incorporate in the mystical body of thy Son, which is the blessed company of all faithful people, and are also heirs through hope of thy everlasting kingdom, by the merits of the most precious death and passion of thy dear Son. And we most humbly beseech thee, O heavenly Father, so to assist us with thy grace, that we may continue in that holy fellowship, and do all such good works as thou hast prepared for us to walk in; through Jesus Christ our Lord, to whom, with thee and the Holy Ghost be all honour and glory, world without end.

The Book of Common Prayer

May our Lord Jesus Christ, whom we have served and celebrated and honoured in his holy, glorious, life-giving and divine mysteries, in his grace and mercy make us worthy of the beauty and glory of his kingdom, and of joy with his holy angels; and to have guiltless faces before him, standing at his right hand in the Jerusalem which is above. To him be praise, and may the right hand of his providence rest upon us and upon all creatures, now and for ever.

Chaldean Liturgy

4.3   Eucharistic Devotions

The following hymns and prayers are traditionally used before the Blessed Sacrament. You may use them in thanksgiving for the Institution of the Eucharist, or before the Sacrament in church.

O salutaris

> O Priest and Victim, Word of Life,
> Throw wide the gates of Paradise.
> We face our foes in mortal strife;
> You are our strength! O heed our cries.
>
> To Father, Son and Spirit blest,
> One only God, be ceaseless praise.
> May you in goodness grant us rest
> In heaven, our home, for endless days.

Tantum ergo

> Come, adore this wondrous presence;
> Bow to Christ, the source of grace.
> Here is kept the ancient promise
> Of God's earthly dwelling place.
> Sight is blind before God's glory,
> Faith alone may see that face.
>
> Glory be to God the Father,
> Praise to his co-equal Son,
> Adoration to the Spirit,
> Bond of love, in Godhead one.
> Blest be God by all creation
> Joyously while ages run.
>
> Your people eat the food of angels
> for you gave them bread from heaven.

Lord Jesus Christ,
we thank you that in a wonderful sacrament
you have given us the memorial of your passion:
grant us so to reverence
the sacred mysteries of your body and blood
that we may know within ourselves
and show forth in our lives the fruits of your redemption;
for you are alive and reign with the Father and the Holy Spirit,
one God, now and for ever. Amen.

A period of silent prayer may be kept.

The Divine Praises

Blessèd be God.
Blessèd be the holy and undivided Trinity.
Blessèd be God the Father, maker of heaven and earth.
Blessèd be Jesus Christ, truly divine and truly human.
Blessèd be the holy Name of Jesus.
Blessèd be Jesus Christ in his death and resurrection.
Blessèd be Jesus Christ on his throne of glory.
Blessèd be Jesus Christ
    in the Sacrament of his body and blood.
Blessèd be God the Holy Spirit, the giver and sustainer of life.
Blessèd be God in the Virgin Mary,
    mother of our Lord and God.
Blessèd be God in his angels and saints.
Blessèd be God.

Psalm 117

Let us adore Christ the Lord in the most holy Sacrament.

O praise the Lord, all you nations;
praise him, all you peoples.

For great is his steadfast love towards us,
and the faithfulness of the Lord endures for ever. Alleluia!

Glory to the Father and to the Son and to the Holy Spirit;
as it was in the beginning is now and shall be for ever. Amen.

Let us adore Christ the Lord in the most holy Sacrament.

5   The Christian Year

For Christians, time is shaped by the Seasons of the Christian year which allow us to recall and relive each year in our prayer and worship what God has done for us in Christ. The year has two groups or cycles of commemorations. The first centres on the Incarnation – how God came among us in Christ to share our life; the second on our Redemption – how God in Christ has transformed that life by his death and resurrection.

The focus of the first cycle is Christmas, when we celebrate the birth of Christ, and it has both a prelude and a period of outworking. Before Christmas comes Advent, when the Church reflects on God's promise to come among his people. Christians celebrate the fulfilment of this promise in the birth of Jesus Christ on Christmas Day, and in the season of Epiphany – the making visible God's coming – we celebrate how this one event has universal significance throughout the world and throughout its history. This cycle ends with the feast of Candlemas, the presentation of Christ in the temple, where old Simeon recognized him as the promised Saviour, and acclaimed him as the light of the world.

Not many weeks later begins the commemoration of our Redemption, focused in the celebrations of Holy Week and Easter. The six weeks of Lent, originally the concentrated time of final preparation for those who were going to be received into the Church and baptized at Easter, begin on Ash Wednesday, a day of fasting and penitence. As we journey with Christ through the forty days of Lent, we have an annual opportunity to renew our discipleship, so that by the time we come to Palm Sunday and Holy Week begins, we are ready to relive the central events of our faith. Maundy Thursday, Good Friday and Holy Saturday are followed by Easter Day, the celebration of the resurrection and the fulcrum of our faith. And like Epiphanytide, Eastertide is a period of sustained rejoicing where the Easter faith can be worked out and put into practice. The day of Pentecost – the fiftieth day – celebrates the moment where the Church had received sufficient confidence to move out and begin to share the good news of what God had done for us in Christ.

Eastertide ends with Pentecost, and we enter a period of the Church's year called Ordinary time. The first Sunday after Pentecost celebrates the Holy Trinity, how we know God as Father, Son and Holy Spirit, and the Sundays after that are all called Sundays after Trinity until the end of the year.

Towards the end of the year come the festival of All Saints and the commemoration of All Souls on 1st and 2nd November. As the year fades, we begin to recall our own mortality, our approaching end, and the sense that as strangers and pilgrims here on earth, our home is in heaven. That gives us the forward impetus to look again for the coming of God's kingdom, and prepares us for the celebration of Advent once again.

The year's calendar is shot through with another thread — the annual commemorations of the saints. Celebrated on the day of their death — their heavenly birthday — saints' days give pinpricks of personal colour to relieve the drab landscape of worthy Christian history. 'God preserve us from sullen saints,' said that down-to-earth Spanish Abbess, Teresa of Avila. And for the most part, that is true. In the New Testament, 'the saints' refer to the whole company of Christian believers, but it was not long before certain qualities — having met the risen Christ or witnessing to him — being a martyr by the manner of your death — began to single out certain individuals. From the time of the apostles up to now the Church as a whole has recognized a quite extraordinary quality of relationship with God in a number of individual Christians. These are the ones whose stories are handed down and whose memory the Church has recognized by calling them 'saints'. As well as being inspired by their examples, Christians find it natural to treat them as their friends, as well as being friends of God. That is why we ask them for their prayers, as we do all our friends.

Chief in this list is the Virgin Mary, whose 'yes' to God was instrumental in our salvation. Her heavenly birthday is celebrated universally on 15th August, but other festivals are related to Christmas Day, with the Annunciation on 25th March, and the Visitation on 31st May; her Nativity falls on 8th September, nine months after her Conception on 8th December. In a category of his own is John the Baptist, whose Nativity — related to Jesus' — is on 24th June, and his death on 29th August.

Then come the feasts of the Apostles, and of the Evangelists. The Martyrs follow, and then come a host of other commemorations, some universally kept and some — like the saints of Cornwall, Wales or Ireland, for example — hardly known outside their own locality.

In this section, there is material first for the Liturgical Seasons of the year. It may be used on its own, to provide seasonal material for daily prayer, or it may be used for seasonal meditation. Then follows material for some of the principal festivals, including saints' days; finally, there are some of the prayers and devotions associated with Our Lady.

5.1   The Incarnation

Advent

Advent is the season of watching and waiting for the coming of God. We recall his promise to come among us in power and great glory, and prepare for his coming in judgement at the end of all things, his coming in the child of Bethlehem in fulfilment of the prophecies of Isaiah and others, and his coming among us now. How shall we recognize him? Will we be caught napping like the foolish virgins? Will we be sheep or goats? Would we — will we — have the nerve to say yes when the angel comes and taps us on the shoulder, like Mary when Gabriel came to her?

In the readings and prayers that follow, we are tuned to attend to the pre-echoes of God's coming. The command to watch and to be ready is common to many of Jesus' parables and sayings. God's coming is like a waterless wilderness springing into life; we need to prepare by putting on the armour of light, or by being fully dressed or having our lamps ready. We need to be alert to recognize God, who comes as judge and saviour.

> The wilderness and the dry land shall rejoice,
> the desert shall blossom and burst into song.
> They shall see the glory of the Lord,
> the majesty of our God.
>
> Strengthen the weary hands,
> and make firm the feeble knees.
> Say to the anxious, 'Be strong, fear not,
> your God is coming with judgement,
> coming with judgement to save you.'
>
> Then shall the eyes of the blind be opened,
> and the ears of the deaf unstopped;
> Then shall the lame leap like a hart,
> and the tongue of the dumb sing for joy.
>
> For waters shall break forth in the wilderness,
> and streams in the desert;
> The ransomed of the Lord shall return with singing,
> with everlasting joy upon their heads.
> Joy and gladness shall be theirs,
> and sorrow and sighing shall flee away.   *Isaiah 35.1,2b—6,10*

A voice cries in the wilderness, 'Prepare the way of the Lord, make straight in the desert a highway for our God. Every valley shall be exalted, and every mountain and hill be brought low; the rough places a plain. And the glory of the Lord shall be revealed, and all flesh shall see it together.'   *Isaiah 40.3–5*

Now it is time for you to wake out of sleep, for salvation is nearer to us now than when we first believed.   *Romans 13.11*

Watch, therefore – for you do not know when the master of the house will come, in the evening or at midnight or at cockcrow, or in the morning – lest he come suddenly and find you asleep. And what I say to you, I say to all: Watch.   *Mark 13.35–36*

Keep us, O Lord, while we tarry on this earth,
in a serious seeking after you
and in an affectionate walking with you,
every day of our lives;
that when you come
we may be found not hiding our talent,
nor serving the flesh,
nor yet asleep with our lamp unfurnished,
but waiting and longing for our Lord,
our glorious God for ever.   *Richard Baxter (1615–1691)*

O Lord our God,
make us watchful and keep us faithful
as we await the coming of your Son our Lord;
that when he shall appear, he may not find us sleeping in sin,
but active in his service and joyful in his praise,
for the glory of your holy name.   *Gelasian Sacramentary*

O Lord,
you have set before us the great hope that your kingdom
        shall come on earth,
and have taught us to pray for its coming;
give us grace to discern the signs of it dawning,
and to work for the perfect day
when your will shall be done on earth as it is in heaven;
through Jesus Christ our Lord.   *Percy Dearmer (1867–1936)*

The Advent Antiphons, meditations on the prophetic titles of the Messiah that were applied to Christ, form the basis of well-known hymns like 'O come, O come Emmanuel'. They may be used one by one in the last week of Advent in Evening Prayer, or as a meditation, or as the basis of an Advent Rosary.

17 December – O Sapientia
O Wisdom, coming forth from the mouth of the Most High,
and reaching mightily from one end of the earth to the other,
ordering all things well:
Come and teach us the way of prudence.

18 December – O Adonai
O Adonai, and leader of the house of Israel,
who appeared to Moses in the fire of the burning bush
and gave him the law on Sinai:
Come and redeem us with an outstretched arm.

19 December – O Radix Jesse
O Root of Jesse, standing as a sign to the people,
before whom kings shall shut their mouths
and whom the nations shall seek:
Come and deliver us and do not delay.

20 December – O Clavis David
O Key of David, and sceptre of the house of Israel,
who opens and no one can shut, shuts and no one can open:
Come and bring the prisoners from the prison house,
who dwell in darkness and the shadow of death.

21 December – O Oriens
O Dayspring, splendour of light eternal and sun of righteousness:
Come and enlighten those who dwell in darkness
and the shadow of death.

22 December – O Rex gentium
O King of the nations, and their desire,
the cornerstone making both one:
Come and save us, whom you formed from the dust.

23 December – O Emmanuel
O Emmanuel, our king and lawgiver,
the desire of all nations and their Saviour:
Come and save us, O Lord our God.

Collect

Almighty God,
give us grace to cast away the works of darkness
and to put on the armour of light,
now in the time of this mortal life,
in which your Son Jesus Christ came to us in great humility;
that on the last day,
when he shall come again in his glorious majesty
to judge the living and the dead,
we may rise to the life immortal;
through him who is alive and reigns with you,
in the unity of the Holy Spirit,
one God, now and for ever. Amen.

A meditation on Nicodemus, who came to Jesus 'by night':

Were all my loud, evil days
Calm and unhaunted as is thy dark tent,
Whose peace but by somé Angel's wing or voice
Is seldom rent;
Then I in heaven all the long year
Would keep, and never wander here.

But living where the sun
Doth all things wake, and where all mix and tire
Themselves and others, I consent and run
To this world's mire,
And by this world's ill-guiding light
Err more than I can do by night.

There is in God, some say,
A deep, but dazzling darkness; as men here
Say it is late and dusky, because they
See not all clear.
O for that night! where I in him
Might live invisible and dim.

Henry Vaughan (1622-1695), an extract from 'The Night'

Yet if His Majesty, our sovereign lord,
Should of his own accord
Friendly himself invite,
And say 'I'll be your guest tomorrow night,'
How we should stir ourselves, call and command
All hands to work! 'Let no man idle stand!

'Set me fine Spanish tables in the hall;
See they be fitted all;
Let there be room to eat
And order taken that there want no meat.
See every sconce and candlestick made bright,
That without tapers they may give a light.

'Look to the presence: are the carpets spread,
The dazie* o'er the head,
The cushions in the chairs,
And all the candles lighted on the stairs?
Perfume the chambers, and in any case
Let each man give attendance in his place!'

Thus, if a king were coming, would we do;
And 'twere good reason too;
For 'tis a duteous thing
To show all honour to an earthly king,
And after all our travail and our cost,
So he be pleased, to think no labour lost.

But at the coming of the King of Heaven
All's set at six and seven;
We wallow in our sin,
Christ cannot find a chamber in the inn.
We entertain Him always like a stranger,
And, as at first, still lodge Him in the manger.

*dazie: canopy   Anon., 16th century

Christmas (25 December)

At Christmas, we celebrate Emmanuel – God with us. This is not the God who comes in cosmic majesty, but the vulnerable newborn child who comes in the particularities of time and space. In Christ, God shares our life that we might come to share his glory.

Where is this stupendous stranger
Prophets, shepherds, kings, advise:
Lead me to my Master's manger,
Show me where my Saviour lies.

O most mighty, O most holy,
Far beyond the seraph's thought!
Art thou then so mean and lowly
As unheeded prophets taught?

O the magnitude of meekness,
Worth from worth immortal sprung!
O the strength of infant weakness,
If eternal is so young!

God all-bounteous, all-creative,
Whom no ills from good dissuade,
Is incarnate – and a native
Of the very world he made.   *Christopher Smart (1722-1771)*

I sing of a maiden

I sing of a maiden   that is makeless
King of all kinges   to her son she ches.

He came all so stille   there his mother was,
As dew in Aprille   that falleth on the grass.

He came all so stille   to his mother's bowr,
As dew in Aprille   that falleth on the flowr

He came all so stille   there his mother lay,
As dew in Aprille   that falleth on the spray.

Mother and maiden   was never none but she;
Well may such a lady   Godes mother be.   *15th century*

Jesus Christ the Apple Tree

The tree of life my soul hath seen,
Laden with fruit, and always green:
The trees of nature fruitless be
Compared with Christ the apple tree.

His beauty doth all things excel:
By faith I know, but ne'er can tell
The glory which I now can see
In Jesus Christ the apple tree.

For happiness I long have sought,
And pleasure dearly I have bought:
I missed of all; but now I see
'Tis found in Christ the apple tree.

I'm weary with my former toil,
Here I will sit and rest awhile:
Under the shadow I will be,
Of Jesus Christ the apple tree.

This fruit doth make my soul to thrive,
It keeps my dying faith alive;
Which makes my soul in haste to be
With Jesus Christ the apple tree.

Anon., collection of Joshua Smith, New Hampshire 1784

When peaceful silence lay over all
and night was in the midst of her swift course:
from your royal throne, O God,
down from the heavens,
leapt your almighty Word!

Antiphon to the Magnificat

Belovèd, let us love one another, because love is from God; everyone who loves is born of God and knows God. Whoever does not love does not know God, for God is love. In this God's love was revealed among us, that God sent his only Son into the world, so that we might live through him. *1 John 4.7–9*

For reflection

The Word was made flesh and dwelt among us, full of grace and truth
and we beheld his glory, the glory of the only begotten of the Father.

John 1.14

Collects

Almighty God, you have given us your only-begotten Son
to take our nature upon him
and as at this time to be born of a pure virgin:
grant that we, who have been born again
and made your children by adoption and grace,
may daily be renewed by your Holy Spirit;
through Jesus Christ our Lord.

Almighty God,
who wonderfully created us in your own image
and yet more wonderfully restored us
through your Son Jesus Christ:
grant that, as he came to share in our humanity,
so we may share the life of his divinity;
who is alive and reigns with you,
in the unity of the Holy Spirit,
one God, now and for ever.

Epiphany (6 January)

The Epiphany, or 'Making public' of Christ's coming follows the Nativity by twelve days in the calendar. But the emphasis is different. In the Western Church, we associate the Epiphany with the visit of the Magi, recorded in Matthew's Gospel. After the private particularity of the birth in a strange place, with rough shepherds summoned by angels as the only witnesses, the coming of the wise men from foreign lands reveals that the newly born is of significance to the whole world, and not just to the local outsiders.

Journey of the Magi

> 'A cold coming we had of it,
> Just the worst time of the year
> For a journey, and such a long journey:
> The ways deep and the weather sharp,
> The very dead of winter.'
> And the camels galled, sore-footed, refractory,
> Lying down in the melted snow.
> There were times we regretted
> The summer palaces on slopes, the terraces,
> And the silken girls bringing sherbet.
> Then the camel men cursing and grumbling
> And running away, and wanting their liquor and women,
> And the night-fires going out, and the lack of shelters,
> And the cities hostile and the towns unfriendly
> And the villages dirty and charging high prices:
> A hard time we had of it.
> At the end we preferred to travel all night,
> Sleeping in snatches,
> With voices singing in our ears, saying
> That this was all folly.

Then at dawn we came down to a temperate valley,
Wet, below the snow line, smelling of vegetation,
With a running stream and a water-mill beating the darkness,
And three trees on the low sky.
And an old white horse galloped away in the meadow.
Then we came to a tavern with vine-leaves over the lintel,
Six hands at an open door dicing for pieces of silver,
And feet kicking the empty wine-skins.
But there was no information, so we continued
And arrived at evening, not a moment too soon
Finding the place; it was (you may say) satisfactory.

All this was a long time ago, I remember,
And I would do it again, but set down
This set down
This: were we led all that way for
Birth or death? There was a Birth, certainly,
We had evidence and no doubt. I had seen birth and death
But had thought they were different; this Birth was
Hard and bitter agony for us, like Death, our death.
We returned to our places, these Kingdoms,
But no longer at ease here, in the old dispensation,
With an alien people clutching their gods.
I should be glad of another death.

T. S. Eliot (1888-1965), Ariel Poems

In the Eastern Church, the visit of the Magi is linked with other significant events:

Three wonders mark this holy day,
as the Church is joined to her heavenly Bridegroom.

This day a star leads the wise men to the manger.
This day water is made wine at the wedding feast.
This day Jesus is revealed as the Christ
    in the waters of baptism. Alleluia.

In the East, this is the main celebration of the Incarnation, and the Blessing of the Waters that accompanies it celebrates the Baptism of Christ, the marriage of earth and heaven, and provides the other principal baptismal season to Eastertide.

Give the king your judgements, O God,
and your righteousness to the son of a king.

Then shall he judge your people righteously
and your poor with justice.

May the mountains bring forth peace,
and the little hills righteousness for the people.

May he defend the poor among the people,
deliver the children of the needy and crush the oppressor.

May he live as long as the sun and moon endure,
from one generation to another.

May he come down like rain upon the mown grass,
like the showers that water the earth.

In his time shall righteousness flourish,
and abundance of peace till the moon shall be no more.

May his dominion extend from sea to sea
and from the River to the ends of the earth.

May his foes kneel before him
and his enemies lick the dust.

All kings shall fall down before him;
all nations shall do him service.

For he shall deliver the poor that cry out,
the needy and those who have no helper.

Long may he live;
    unto him may be given gold from Sheba;
may prayer be made for him continually
    and may they bless him all the day long.

From Psalm 72

A Song of the New Jerusalem

Arise, shine out, for your light has come,
the glory of the Lord is rising upon you.

Though night still covers the earth,
and darkness the peoples;

Above you the Holy One arises,
and above you God's glory appears.

The nations will come to your light,
and kings to your dawning brightness.

No more will the sun give you daylight,
nor moonlight shine upon you;

But the Lord will be your everlasting light,
your God will be your splendour.

From Isaiah 60

We proclaim not ourselves but Christ Jesus as Lord and ourselves as
your servants for Jesus' sake. For it is the God who said, 'Let light
shine out of darkness' who has shone in our hearts to give the light of
the knowledge of the glory of God in the face of Jesus Christ.

2 Corinthians 4.5–7

Collect O God, who by the leading of a star
manifested your only Son to the peoples of the earth:
mercifully grant that we, who know you now by faith,
may at last behold your glory face to face;
through Jesus Christ our Lord.

On the first miracle at Cana in Galilee

The conscious water saw its God and blushed.

Richard Crashaw (1613–1649)

The Baptism of Christ – First Sunday of Epiphany

The Baptism of Christ is recorded in all the Gospels, and is how St Mark's Gospel begins.

> Jesus came from Nazareth of Galilee and was baptized by John in the Jordan. And just as he was coming up out of the water, he saw the heavens torn apart and the Spirit descending like a dove on him. And a voice came from heaven, 'You are my Son, the Belovèd; with you I am well pleased.' *Mark 1.9–11*

These words unite a quotation from Psalm 2, a coronation psalm, and Isaiah 42.1, one of the Suffering Servant songs in which the deliverer of Israel is identified as one who suffers for the whole people. Here Jesus' ministry as the royal son of his Father who will bear the sins of the people is revealed, and our baptism, signed with the cross — the badge of suffering — and anointed as his royal, priestly people is prefigured.

> John said, 'Behold the Lamb of God, who takes away the sin of the world.' *John 1.29*

A Song of Deliverance

> 'Behold, God is my salvation;
> I will trust and will not be afraid;

> 'For the Lord God is my strength and my song,
> and has become my salvation.'

> With joy you will draw water
> from the wells of salvation.

> On that day you will say,
> 'Give thanks to the Lord, call upon his name;

> 'Make known his deeds among the nations,
> proclaim that his name is exalted.

> 'Sing God's praises, who has triumphed gloriously;
> let this be known in all the world.

> 'Shout and sing for joy, you that dwell in Zion,
> for great in your midst is the Holy One of Israel.'
>
> *Isaiah 12. 2–6*

John testified: 'I saw the Spirit descending from heaven like a dove, and it remained on him. I myself did not know him but the one who sent me to baptize with water said to me, "He on whom you see the Spirit descend and remain is the one who baptizes with the Holy Spirit."'

John 1.32,33

At the Blessing of the Waters

Let us give thanks to the Lord our God.
All　*It is right to give thanks and praise.*

It is indeed right, it is our duty and our joy
at all times to give you thanks and praise,
for today the grace of the Holy Spirit
in the form of a dove descended upon the waters.

Today the sun that never sets has risen
and the world is filled with splendour
by the light of the Lord.
Today the clouds drop down upon mankind
the dew of righteousness from on high.
Today the Uncreated of his own will
accepts the laying on of hands from his own creature.
Today the waters of the Jordan
are transformed for healing by the coming of the Lord.
Today our transgressions are washed away
by the waters of the river.
Today the blinding mist of the world is dispersed
by the Epiphany of our God.
Today things above keep feast with things below,
and things below commune with things above.

Therefore, heavenly Father,
accept our sacrifice of praise,
and by the power of your life-giving Spirit
sanctify these waters of your new creation,
that we, with all who have been born anew
by water and the Spirit,
may be renewed in your image,
walk by the light of faith,
and serve you in newness of life.
Through your anointed Son, Jesus Christ our Lord,
to whom with you and the Holy Spirit
we lift our voices of praise:

All *Blessed be God, our strength and our salvation,*
now and for ever. Amen.

Collect Eternal Father,
who at the baptism of Jesus revealed him to be your Son,
anointing him with the Holy Spirit:
grant to us, who are born again by water and the Spirit,
that we may be faithful to our calling as your adopted children;
through Jesus Christ our Lord.

Candlemas (2 February)

The celebration of Candlemas – The Presentation of Christ in the Temple, and his recognition there by old Simeon and Anna as the Light of the World – marks the end of the annual celebration of the Incarnation which began at Advent. The Gospel for the festival is Luke 2.22–38. We pray that we too may recognize the Christ when we meet him, and do not forget our responsibility for holding his light before the world.

For this day also of his presentation, as well as those others of his birth, circumcision and manifestation – Candlemas day as well as Christmas day, New Year's day, or Epiphany, is a day of blessing; a day of God's blessing us, and our blessing to him again; of Christ's being presented to us, and our presenting to him again; of his presenting in the temple, and our presenting ourselves in the Church, to bless God and him for his presentation, his presentation-day and our Candlemas, our little candles, or petty lights, our souls reflecting back to his great light, that was this day presented in the temple and then darted down upon us.

From a Candlemas Sermon by Mark Frank 1613–1664

See, I am sending my messenger to prepare the way before me, and the Lord whom you seek will suddenly come to his temple. The messenger of the covenant in whom you delight – indeed, he is coming, says the Lord of hosts. But who can endure the day of his coming, and who can stand when he appears? For he is like a refiner's fire and like fullers' soap; he will sit as a refiner and purifier of silver, and he will purify the descendants of Levi and refine them like gold and silver, until they present offerings to the Lord in righteousness. Then the offering of Judah and Jerusalem will be pleasing to the Lord as in the days of old and as in former years.

Malachi 3.1–4

Now, Lord, you let your servant go in peace:
your word has been fulfilled.
My own eyes have seen the salvation
which you have prepared in the sight of every people;
A light to reveal you to the nations
and the glory of your people Israel.

Luke 2.29–32

The Blessing of the Candles

Lord God, the springing source of everlasting light,
pour into the hearts of your faithful people
the brilliance of your eternal splendour,
that we, who by these kindling flames
light up this temple to your glory,
may have the darkness of our souls dispelled,
and so be counted worthy to stand before you
in that eternal temple where you live and reign
Father, Son, and Holy Spirit,
one God, now and for ever.

For reflection

We wait for your loving-kindness, O God,
in the midst of your temple.

Collect Almighty and ever-living God,
clothed in majesty,
whose belovèd Son was this day presented in the Temple,
in substance of our flesh:
grant that we may be presented to you
with pure and clean hearts,
by your Son Jesus Christ our Lord.

From the giving of a lighted candle in the baptism service

You have received the light of Christ;
walk in this light all the days of your life.

Shine as a light in the world
to the glory of God the Father.

Go in the light and peace of Christ.
Thanks be to God.

5.2   Our Redemption

Ash Wednesday

Lent begins on Ash Wednesday, a day of penitence and fasting. The liturgy of the day includes a significant penitential element, and is one of the days when the Penitential rite may follow the Gospel and Sermon. The distinctive element is the marking on each person's forehead of a cross in ash, made from the embers of last year's palm crosses, with the chilling words:

> Remember that you are dust, and to dust you shall return.
>
> *Genesis 3.19b*

The palms of victory with which we celebrated our allegiance to Jesus our king have turned to dust and ashes in our disloyalty: we start again in the dust of 'man's first disobedience'.

> Jesus said, 'When you fast, anoint your head and wash your face, so that your fasting may be seen not by others but by your Father who is in secret.'
>
> *Matthew 6.17–18*

For reflection
> Create in me a clean heart, O God,
> And renew a right spirit within me.

Collect Almighty and everlasting God,
> Who hatest nothing that thou hast made,
> and dost forgive the sins of all them that are penitent:
> Create and make in us new and contrite hearts
> that we worthily lamenting our sins,
> and acknowledging our wretchedness,
> may obtain of thee, the God of all mercy,
> perfect remission and forgiveness;
> through Jesus Christ our Lord.

Lent

Lent, originally the season for intense preparation for the candidates for baptism at Easter, has retained something of this character as a time for growth in the faith and renewal, and it is good to begin with a realistic assessment of where we stand. The name 'Shrove Tuesday' comes from the old word 'to shrive', to absolve someone from their sins, and the start of Lent is a moment to take sin and its remedy seriously (see Chapter 6, p.199).

Is this a fast, to keep
  The larder lean?
    And clean
From fat of veals, and sheep?

Is it to quit the dish
  Of Flesh, yet still
    To fill
The platter high with fish?

Is it to fast an hour,
  Or ragged to go,
    Or show
A down-cast look, and sour?

No: 'tis a fast, to dole
  Thy sheaf of wheat
    And meat
Unto the hungry soul.

It is to fast from strife,
  From old debate,
    And hate;
To circumcise thy life.

To show a heart grief-rent;
  To starve thy sin,
    Not bin;
And that's to keep thy Lent.

Robert Herrick (1592-1674)

Have mercy on me, O God, in your great goodness;
according to the abundance of your compassion blot out my offences.

Wash me thoroughly from my wickedness
and cleanse me from my sin.

For I acknowledge my faults
and my sin is ever before me.

Against you only have I sinned
and done what is evil in your sight,

So that you are justified in your sentence
and righteous in your judgement.

I have been wicked even from my birth,
a sinner when my mother conceived me.

Behold, you desire truth deep within me
and shall make me understand wisdom in the depths of my heart.

Purge me with hyssop and I shall be clean;
wash me and I shall be whiter than snow.

Make me hear of joy and gladness,
that the bones you have broken may rejoice.

Turn your face from my sins
and blot out all my misdeeds.

Make me a clean heart, O God,
and renew a right spirit within me.

Cast me not away from your presence
and take not your holy spirit from me.

Give me again the joy of your salvation
and sustain me with your gracious spirit;

Then shall I teach your ways to the wicked
and sinners shall return to you.

Deliver me from my guilt, O God, the God of my salvation,
and my tongue shall sing of your righteousness.

O Lord, open my lips
and my mouth shall proclaim your praise.

For you desire no sacrifice, else I would give it;
you take no delight in burnt offerings.

The sacrifice of God is a broken spirit;
a broken and contrite heart, O God, you will not despise.

O be favourable and gracious to Zion;
build up the walls of Jerusalem.

Then you will accept sacrifices offered in righteousness,
  the burnt offerings and oblations;
then shall they offer up bulls on your altar.

Psalm 51

Lord Jesus think on me,
And purge away my sin;
From earthbound passions set me free,
And make me pure within.

Lord Jesus think on me,
With care and woe opprest;
Let me thy loving servant be,
And taste thy promised rest.

Lord Jesus think on me,
Amid the battle's strife;
In all my pain and misery
Be thou my health and life.

Lord Jesus think on me,
Nor let me go astray;
Through darkness and perplexity
Point thou the heavenly way.

Lord Jesus think on me,
When flows the tempest high;
When on doth rush the enemy
O Saviour, be thou nigh.

Lord Jesus think on me,
That when the flood is past,
I may the eternal brightness see
And share thy joy at last.

Bishop Synesius (375–430), tr. A. W. Chatfield

Passiontide

My song is love unknown,
  my Saviour's love to me,
love to the loveless shown,
  that they might lovely be.
    O who am I,
      that for my sake
      my Lord should take
    frail flesh, and die?

He came from his blest throne,
  salvation to bestow;
but men made strange, and none
  the longed-for Christ would know.
    But O, my Friend,
      my Friend indeed,
      who at my need
    his life did spend!

Sometimes they strew his way,
  and his sweet praises sing;
resounding all the day
  Hosannas to their King.
    Then 'Crucify!'
      is all their breath,
      and for his death
    they thirst and cry.

Why, what hath my Lord done?
  What makes this rage and spite?
He made the lame to run,
  he gave the blind their sight.
    Sweet injuries!
      Yet they at these
      themselves displease,
    And 'gainst him rise.

They rise, and needs will have
  my dear Lord made away;
a murderer they save,
  the Prince of Life they slay.
      Yet cheerful he
        to suffering goes,
        that he his foes
      from thence might free.

In life, no house, no home
  my Lord on earth might have;
in death, no friendly tomb
  but what a stranger gave.
      What may I say?
        Heaven was his home;
        but mine the tomb
      wherein he lay.

Here might I stay and sing:
  no story so divine;
never was love, dear King,
  never was grief like thine!
      This is my Friend,
        in whose sweet praise
        I all my days
      could gladly spend.

Samuel Crossman (1624-1683)

He was despised and rejected, a man of sorrows and acquainted with grief; and as one from whom others hide their faces he was despised, and we held him of no account. Surely he has borne our griefs and carried our sorrows; yet we accounted him stricken, struck down by God, and afflicted. But he was wounded for our transgressions, bruised for our iniquities; and upon him was the punishment that made us whole, and by his stripes we are healed.

Isaiah 53.3—5

Jesus said, 'I am the good shepherd. The good shepherd lays down his life for the sheep. The hired hand, who is not the shepherd and does not own the sheep, sees the wolf coming and leaves the sheep and runs away — and the wolf snatches them and scatters them. I am the good shepherd. I know my own and my own know me, just as the Father knows me and I know the Father. And I lay down my life for the sheep.'

John 10.11—15

Christ leads me through no darker rooms
than he went through before.

Richard Baxter(1615-1691), 'Lord, it belongs not to my care'

The Stations of the Cross

If you go to Jerusalem on pilgrimage, you will be invited to follow the Via Dolorosa. There, in the streets of Jerusalem, the tradition of walking the Stations of the Cross continues. When the Holy places became inaccessible at the time of the Crusades, the tradition of following the footsteps of Christ was translated, with much of the Holy Week ritual, to the local church. Round the walls of the church, especially during Lent and Passiontide, are set fourteen representations of the Way of the Cross. In some churches in the Middle Ages a Labyrinth or maze was placed in the floor of the nave of the church for penitents and would-be pilgrims to follow on their knees.

At each of the Stations, you may use the following prayers:

> We adore you, O Christ, and we bless you:
> because by your holy cross you have redeemed the world.
>
> > Holy God,
> > Holy and strong,
> > Holy and immortal,
> > have mercy upon us.
>
> Lord Jesus Christ, Son of the living God,
> have mercy on me, a sinner.

At the end, you may use these prayers:

> > Lord, have mercy upon us.
> > Christ, have mercy upon us.
> > Lord, have mercy upon us
>
> > Our Father ...
>
> > Lord Jesus Christ, Son of the living God,
> > set your passion, cross and death between your judgement and us,
> > now and at the hour of our death.
> > Give mercy and grace to the living, rest to the departed,
> > to your holy Church peace and concord,
> > and to us sinners life eternal and glory;
> > for you are alive and reign with the Father and the Holy Spirit,
> > one God, now and for ever.

From None

I   *Jesus is condemned to death*

Lord Jesus, you were innocent, yet you consented to suffer for me.
I am guilty: bring me to hate my sins and accept your forgiveness.

II   *Jesus receives the cross*

Jesus, grant me strength to face the trials of my calling as a Christian,
and be ready to take up my cross and follow you.

III   *Jesus falls the first time*

Jesus, you bore the weight of my sins on your cross;
release me from that burden, that I may not stumble.

IV   *Jesus meets his mother*

Jesus, when you met your mother you recognized the anguish of her heart;
may we be ready to love without restraint, even when the sword pierces our
own heart also.

V   *The cross is laid on Simon of Cyrene*

Jesus, you accepted the help of a stranger in bearing your cross;
may I be ready to accept the help others willingly offer me.

VI   *Veronica wipes Jesus' face*

Lord Jesus, you left the imprint of your sorrows on Veronica's cloth;
imprint your love upon my heart, that one day I may see you face to face.

VII   *Jesus falls a second time*

Jesus, falling under the weight of the world's sin,
help me to lift you up, so that you may draw all your children to yourself.

VIII   *The women of Jerusalem weep for our Lord*

As the women of Jerusalem were moved by your sufferings,
    though they did not know you,
help us, loving Jesus, to be moved to action by the suffering
    of those we do not know.

IX   *Jesus falls a third time*

Lord, as you fall into the dust from which we are made,
may I never feel so unloved as to fall utterly from you.

x   *Jesus is stripped of his garments*

Strip me, Lord, I pray, of all the trappings of power and success
beneath which I try to hide the naked ambition and love of self
    which cripples me.

XI   *Jesus is nailed to the cross*

Lord Jesus Christ, nailed to the cross for me;
draw me into your wounds that I may be made one with you,
    in life and in death.

XII   *Jesus dies on the cross*

Jesus, in dying for me you completed the work of my salvation;
may I rejoice in the power of your victory, and praise you for my new life.

XIII   *Jesus is laid in his mother's arms*

Mary, mother of Christ, you held in your arms once again the Saviour
    of the world;
pray that he may receive me into his loving arms, now and at the hour
    of my death.

XIV   *Jesus is buried in the sepulchre*

Lord Jesus Christ, as your body rested in the grave, hallowing it for my
    new birth,
make me ready to die daily to sin and prepare me for life in all its fullness.

Holy Week

Although the earliest celebration of the Christian Pasch was a single liturgy spanning both death and resurrection, the practice of historicizing each event throughout the Great Week was already in place by the time the Spanish nun, Egeria, visited Jerusalem from 381 to 384. She describes in some detail where the events took place, what passages were read and what ceremony marked the moment. Much of our Holy Week Liturgy derives from this sense of a dramatic unfolding of the events.

Palm Sunday

Holy Week begins with the processional entry into the church, which becomes Jerusalem for the week. The Procession with branches, banners and flags — more important than the blessing and distribution of little palm crosses as a keepsake — starts outside, in some public space. The procession has the character of a noisy demonstration in praise of Christ the king, but those who welcome Christ with shouts of 'Hosanna' will find themselves shouting 'crucify him' in the dramatic reading of the Passion (traditionally St Matthew's account) a few moments later in the liturgy.

> The crowds that went ahead of Jesus and that followed were shouting, 'Hosanna to the Son of David! Blessèd is he who comes in the name of the Lord! Hosanna in the highest heaven!' When he entered Jerusalem, the whole city was in turmoil, asking, 'Who is this?'
>
> *Matthew 21.9—10*

Collect Almighty and everlasting God,
who, of thy tender love towards mankind,
hast sent thy Son, our Saviour Jesus Christ,
to take upon him our flesh,
and to suffer death upon the cross,
that all mankind should follow the example of his great humility;
mercifully grant that we may both follow the example of his patience,
and also be made partakers of his resurrection;
through the same Jesus Christ our Lord.

Maundy Thursday

On Maundy Thursday the Church celebrates the inauguration at the Last Supper of the Eucharist. But there are other commemorations surrounding that. In the cathedral that morning, the bishop may have gathered the clergy and other ministers of the diocese to bless the Oils that will be used at Easter and to pray for one another as they prepare to lead the Church's worship in the Triduum, the three holy days. That evening, the celebration includes a dramatic representation of the Gospel (John 13.1–15) when the priest washes the feet of members of the congregation, enrolling them in Jesus' ministry of service. At the end of the liturgy, the Sacrament is carried to an altar where a Watch is kept, giving us an opportunity to 'watch and pray' with Jesus in the Garden of Gethsemane.

For I received from the Lord what I also delivered to you, that the Lord Jesus on the night when he was betrayed took bread, and when he had given thanks, he broke it, and said, 'This is my body which is for you. Do this in remembrance of me.' In the same way also the cup, after supper, saying, 'This cup is the new covenant in my blood. Do this, as often as you drink it, in remembrance of me.' For as often as you eat this bread and drink this cup, you proclaim the Lord's death until he comes.   *1 Corinthians 11.23–26*

Collect Lord Jesus Christ,
we thank you that in a wonderful sacrament
you have given us the memorial of your passion:
grant us so to reverence
the sacred mysteries of your body and blood
that we may know within ourselves
and show forth in our lives the fruits of your redemption;
for you are alive and reign with the Father and the Holy Spirit,
one God, now and for ever.

At the washing of feet

Jesus said, 'If I, your Lord and Teacher, have washed your feet, you also ought to wash one another's feet. For I have set you an example, that you also should do as I have done to you.'
                John 13.14–15

For reflection

Ubi caritas et amor, Deus ibi est.
Where love and charity are, there is God himself.

Collect Jesus, Lord and Master, who served your disciples
in washing their feet;
serve us often, serve us daily, in washing our motives, our ambitions,
our actions;
that we may share with you in your mission to the world
and serve others gladly for your sake;
to whom be glory for ever.

After Michael Ramsey (1904-1988)

In the garden of Gethsemane

And going a little farther, Jesus fell on the ground and prayed ...
'Abba, Father, all things are possible to thee; remove this cup from me;
yet not what I will, but what thou wilt.' *Mark 14.35,36*

My heart is disquieted within me,
and the terrors of death have fallen upon me.
Fearfulness and trembling are come upon me,
and a horrible dread has overwhelmed me.
And I said: 'O that I had wings like a dove,
for then would I fly away and be at rest.
Then would I flee far away
and make my lodging in the wilderness.'

For it was not an open enemy that reviled me,
for then I could have borne it;
Nor was it my adversary that puffed himself up against me,
for then I would have hid myself from him.
But it was even you, one like myself,
my companion and my own familiar friend.
We took sweet counsel together
and walked with the multitude in the house of God.

My companion stretched out his hands against his friend
and has broken his covenant;
His speech was softer than butter, though war was in his heart;
his words were smoother than oil, yet are they naked swords.
Cast your burden upon the Lord and he will sustain you,
and will not let the righteous fall for ever.

Psalm 55.5-8,13-16,22-24

Collect Lord Jesus Christ, Son of the living God,
set your passion, cross and death between your judgement and us,
now and at the hour of our death.
Give mercy and grace to the living, rest to the departed,
to your holy Church peace and concord,
and to us sinners life eternal and glory;
for you are alive and reign with the Father and the Holy Spirit,
one God, now and for ever.

From None

Good Friday

*While popular devotion — whether the Jesuit-inspired Three Hours Devotion or the
Stations of the Cross — concentrates on identifying with the sufferings of Christ, the
Liturgy of Good Friday celebrates the triumph of the cross. The Gospel is the Passion
according to John, where the cross is seen as the moment where God's glory is revealed,
and the whole world is drawn to worship at the foot of the cross.*

'I, if I am lifted up, will draw all people to myself.'

John 12.20

*This triumph is announced in Jesus' dying words — τετελεσται — 'it is finished', or,
more accurately: 'it is perfectly accomplished'. In John's Gospel, Jesus hands over his
Spirit to the core of his Church, his mother, Mary, and John, his beloved disciple, with a
cry of triumphal achievement that echoes the satisfaction of the Creator in Genesis 1.20.
By the fruit of the tree of death, freely given, the human race's old disobedience and
consequent loss of life is reversed. So in the liturgy, after the reading of the Passion, the
cross is set up for veneration. The ancient hymn, 'Sing, my tongue the glorious battle',
rehearses the triumph of our salvation history, and the use of Psalm 67 gives a universal
quality to the promise of salvation.*

Collect Almighty God,
we beseech thee graciously to behold this thy family,
for which our Lord Jesus Christ was contented to be betrayed,
and given up into the hands of wicked men,
and to suffer death upon the cross,
who now liveth and reigneth with thee and the Holy Ghost,
ever one God, world without end.

Pange, lingua, gloriosi proelium certaminis

Sing, my tongue, the glorious battle,
    Sing the ending of the fray;
Now above the Cross, the trophy,
    Sound the loud triumphal lay:
Tell how Christ, the world's redeemer,
    As a victim won the day.

God in pity saw man fallen,
    Shamed and sunk in misery,
When he fell on death by tasting
    Fruit of the forbidden tree;
Then another tree was chosen
    Which the world from death should free.

Thus the scheme of our salvation
    Was of old in order laid,
That the manifold deceiver's
    Art by art might be outweighed,
And the lure the foe put forward
    Into means of healing made.

Therefore when the appointed fullness
    Of the holy time was come,
He was sent who maketh all things
    Forth from God's eternal home;
Thus he came to earth, incarnate,
    Offspring of a maiden's womb.

Thirty years among us dwelling,
    His appointed time fulfilled,
Born for this, he meets his Passion,
    For that this he freely willed,
On the Cross the lamb is lifted
    Where his lifeblood shall be spilled.

He endured the nails, the spitting,
  Vinegar, and spear and reed;
From that holy Body broken
  Blood and water forth proceed:
Earth, and stars, and sky, and ocean
  By that flood from stain are freed.

Faithful Cross! above all other,
  One and only noble tree!
None in foliage, none in blossom,
  None in fruit thy peer may be;
Sweetest wood and sweetest iron!
  Sweetest weight is hung on thee.

Bend thy boughs, O Tree of Glory!
  Thy relaxing sinews bend;
For awhile the ancient rigour
  That thy birth bestowed, suspend;
And the King of heavenly beauty
  On thy bosom gently tend.

Thou alone wast counted worthy
  This world's ransom to uphold;
For a shipwreck'd race preparing
  Harbour, like the ark of old;
With the sacred blood anointed
  From the smitten lamb that rolled.

To the Trinity be glory
  Everlasting, as is meet;
Equal to the Father, equal
  To the Son and Paraclete;
Trinal Unity, whose praises
  All created things repeat.

Venantius Fortunatus (530-609)

The prayers that follow are prayers you may use on any Friday, whenever you want to recall Good Friday and join your prayer for the world's sufferings with Christ's perpetual intercession to the Father. On the cross, Jesus offered himself to the Father for the whole world. At the foot of his cross, we join our prayers with his.

When you go forward to venerate the cross on Good Friday, you may kiss the wood, or lay your forehead on it as a sign of entrusting to God, in union with Christ and his suffering, your own burdens as well as those of others. If you are on your own, it may help to lay a crucifix on the floor, or set five red lights out in a cross-shape before you.

We adore you, O Christ, and we bless you:
because by your holy cross
you have redeemed the world.

> Holy God,
> Holy and strong,
> Holy and immortal,
> have mercy upon us.

We glory in your cross, O Lord,
and praise and glorify your holy resurrection:
for by virtue of the cross,
joy has come to the whole world.

> God be gracious to us and bless us
> and make his face to shine upon us,
> that your way may be known upon earth,
> your saving power among all nations.

We glory in your cross, O Lord,
and praise and glorify your holy resurrection:
for by virtue of the cross,
joy has come to the whole world.

Lord, by this sweet and saving sign,
Defend us from our foes and thine.

Jesu, by thy wounded feet,
　Direct our path aright;
Jesu, by thy nailed hands,
　Move ours to deeds of love;
Jesu, by thy pierced side,
　Cleanse our desires;
Jesu, by thy crown of thorns,
　Annihilate our pride;
Jesu, by thy silence,
　Shame our complaints;
Jesu, by thy parched lips,
　Curb our cruel speech;
Jesu, by thy closing eyes,
　Look on our sin no more;
Jesu, by thy broken heart,
　Knit ours to thine.

And by this sweet and saving sign,
Lord, draw us to our peace, and thine.

Richard Crashaw (1613–1649) and others

May the life-giving cross be the source of all our joy and peace,
and may some fruit from the Tree of thy Passsion
fall on us, O Lord, this day.

For reflection

Christ Jesus emptied himself, taking the form of a servant,
being born in human likeness; and being found in human form,
he humbled himself and became obedient to the point of death,
even death on a cross.

Philippians 2.7–8

The wounded surgeon plies the steel
That questions the distempered part;
Beneath the bleeding hands we feel
The sharp compassion of the healer's art
Resolving the enigma of the fever chart.

Our only health is the disease
If we obey the dying nurse
Whose constant care is not to please
But to remind of our, and Adam's curse
And that, to be restored, our sickness must grow worse.

The whole earth is our hospital
Endowed by the ruined millionaire,
Wherein, if we do well, we shall
Die of the absolute paternal care
That will not leave us, but prevents us everywhere.

The chill ascends from feet to knees,
The fever sings in mental wires.
If to be warmed, then I must freeze
And quake in frigid purgatorial fires
Of which the flame is roses, and the smoke is briars.

The dripping blood our only drink,
The bloody flesh our only food:
In spite of which we like to think
That we are sound, substantial flesh and blood –
Again, in spite of that, we call this Friday good.

T. S. Eliot (1888-1965), an extract from 'East Coker'

The Welsh priest and poet R. S. Thomas uses the image of a musical instrument in his poem 'The Musician', as does George Herbert in his poem 'Easter' on p.159.

The Musician

> A memory of Kreisler once:
> At some recital in this same city,
> The seats all taken, I found myself pushed
> On to the stage with a few others,
> So near that I could see the toil
> Of his face muscles, a pulse like a moth
> Fluttering under the fine skin,
> And the indelible veins of his smooth brow.
>
> I could see, too, the twitching of the fingers,
> Caught temporarily in art's neurosis,
> As we sat there or warmly applauded
> This player who so beautifully suffered
> For each of us upon his instrument.
>
> So it must have been on Calvary
> In the fiercer light of the thorns' halo:
> The men standing by and that one figure,
> The hands bleeding, the mind bruised but calm,
> Making such music as lives still.
> And no one daring to interrupt
> Because it was himself that he played
> And closer than all of them the God listened.

R. S. Thomas (1913-2001)

Easter Eve *or* Holy Saturday

This is a non-day, a time of silent waiting, hardly daring to breathe. There is a tradition which says that between the observance of the Lord's burial and the kindling of the new fire that marks the start of Easter, the church remains silent too. Waiting alone in the darkness of a gothic church, with the ribs of the vaulting arching above you like the ribs of some great beached whale, you can pray the prayer of Jonah from the belly of the great fish.

I called to you, O God, out of my distress
and you answered me;
out of the belly of Sheol I cried,
and you heard my voice.

You cast me into the deep,
into the heart of the seas,
and the flood surrounded me,
all your waves and billows passed over me.

Then I said, I am driven away from your sight;
how shall I ever look again upon your holy temple?

The waters closed in over me,
the deep was round about me;
weeds were wrapped around my head
at the roots of the mountains.

I went down to the land
whose bars closed upon me for ever,
yet you brought up my life from the depths, O God.

As my life was ebbing away, I remembered you, O God,
and my prayer came to you, into your holy temple.

With the voice of thanksgiving, I will sacrifice to you;
what I have vowed I will pay;
deliverance belongs to the Lord!

From Jonah 2

Jesus said, 'Destroy this temple, and in three days I will raise it up.'
This he said of the temple that was his body.

John 2.19,21

Collect Grant, O Lord, that we who are baptized into the death
of thy blessed Son our Saviour Jesus Christ,
may continually put to death our evil desires
and be buried with him;
and that through the grave and gate of death
we may pass to our joyful resurrection;
through his merits,
who died and was buried and rose again for us,
your Son Jesus Christ our Lord.

Eastertide

While we may long to know 'Who moved the stone?', it was the ones who had met the risen Christ, the apostolic witnesses to the resurrection, who were held in honour, Mary Magdalene holding pride of place among them. Luke's account of the journey to Emmaus is deeply significant for the Church's life: the risen Christ meets each worshipper in the breaking of the bread.

But what happened in the darkness of the tomb? We do not know, which is why the church holds its breath on Holy Saturday, waiting. But in Christian imagination, there takes place the crucial conflict between life and death — The Harrowing of Hell, as it became known in the medieval Mystery Plays. And this is how the resurrection is always depicted in icons, with Christ emerging triumphant from the jaws of hell, stepping over the broken bars and shattered locks, leading Adam by one hand and Eve with the other.

This account of the Easter Vigil in Greece captures some of the flavour of the drama.

Easter, in the Orthodox Church, far surpasses in importance all other feasts, and in Greece it is celebrated by the whole nation, including even those who for the rest of the year are notoriously indifferent in such matters, with a fervour and intensity considerably greater than that which we are accustomed to display at Christmas. The fast of Lent has been observed in progressive stages, culminating, in Holy Week, for the devout in almost total abstinence and in an absence of meat even on the mondaine dinner tables of Kolanaki. All Good Friday the bells have tolled ceaselessly from every belfry in Athens, and after dark the Bier has been carried in procession round the confines of every parish. Holy Saturday is a *dies non*; for the only time in the whole year the cafés are empty and even the terrace at Yennaki's is deserted except for a handful of foreigners, while in the church all is dark save for one solitary candle on the altar. Towards midnight the space opposite the great west doors of the Metropolis, and of every church throughout the land, is gradually filled by an immense crowd in whom the fasting of the previous week and the unaccustomed gloom of the day, so foreign to the nature of a people not markedly austere, have induced a nervous condition bordering on hysteria. The wooden platform erected on a line with the high altar is now occupied by members of the government and representatives of the diplomatic corps, the latter holding their candles in the slightly embarrassed manner of grown ups participating in a game of oranges and lemons, while from the open doors the sound of the chanting which has been going on within the darkened cathedral for many hours takes on a more urgent note. A few minutes before midnight the Archbishop emerges attended by two deacons, one carrying a lighted candle from the altar, and mounting the platform begins the reading of the Gospel. By now a deathly hush, or what passes in Greece for a deathly hush, that is to say an absence of sound that compares not unfavourably with the noise of the small mammal-house on a quiet afternoon, has fallen on the vast crowd, which is maintained unbroken until, on the stroke of midnight, the Bishop pronounces the words 'Χριστος 'ανεστη,' 'Christ is risen'. At this the night is rent by a wave of sound in comparison with which all the noises to which one has grown accustomed on other days of the year are as tinkling cymbals. A massed choir and two brass bands burst into powerful, though different, songs of praise; the guard of honour presents arms with a crash unrivalled even in the Wellington Barracks; every bell in the city, ably assisted by air-raid syrens and factory whistles, clangs out the good news, while the cheering crowds greet their Risen Lord with a barrage of rockets, squibs, Roman candles, Chinese crackers, and volley after volley of small-arms fire discharged by such of the devout, a not inconsiderable proportion, as have come to the ceremony armed.

From Osbert Lancaster, Classical Landscape with Figures

The experience of meeting the risen Christ takes place in a garden. The second Adam comes to the rescue and reverses the loss of our immortality and the expulsion from paradise, the result of the first Adam's sin. So where life was lost, there life has been restored and the new creation begins, like the first, in a garden.

But Mary stood weeping outside the tomb, and as she wept, she stooped to look into the tomb; and she saw two angels in white where the body of Jesus had lain, one at the head and one at the feet. And they said to her, 'Woman, why are you weeping?' She said to them, 'Because they have taken away my Lord, and I do not know where they have laid him.' Saying this, she turned round and saw Jesus standing, but she did not know that it was Jesus.

John 20.11–14

Under the dark trees, there he stands,
There he stands; shall he not draw my eyes?
I thought I knew a little
How he compels, beyond all things, but now
He stands there in the shadows. It will be
Oh, such a daybreak, such bright morning,
When I shall wake to see him
As he is.

He is called Rose of Sharon, for his skin
Is clear, his skin is flushed with blood,
His body lovely and exact; how he compels
Beyond ten thousand rivals. There he stands,
My friend, the friend of guilt and helplessness,
To steer my hollow body
Over the sea.

The earth is full of masks and fetishes,
What is there here for me? Are these like him?
Keep company with him and you will know:
No kin, no likeness to those empty eyes.
He is a stranger to them all, great Jesus.
What is there here for me? I know
What I have longed for. Him to hold
Me always.

From the Welsh of Ann Griffiths (1776-1805),
tr. Rowan Williams (1950-)

Rise heart; thy Lord is risen. Sing his praise
        Without delayes,
Who takes thee by the hand, that thou likewise
        With him mayest rise;
That as his death calcined thee to dust,
His life may make thee gold, and much more just.

Awake, my lute, and struggle for thy part
        With all thy art.
The crosse taught all wood to resound his name,
        Who bore the same.
His stretched sinews taught all strings, what key
Is best to celebrate this most high day.

Consort both heart and lute, and twist a song
        Pleasant and long:
Or since all musick is but three parts vied
        And multiplied;
O let thy blessed Spirit bear a part,
And make up our defects with his sweet art.

I got me flowers to straw thy way;
I got me boughs off many a tree:
But thou wast up by break of day,
And brought'st thy sweets along with thee.

The sunne arising in the East,
Though he give light, & th'East perfume;
If they should offer to contest
With thy arising, they presume.

Can there be any day but this,
Though many sunnes to shine endeavour?
We count three hundred, but we misse:
There is but one, and that one ever.

George Herbert (1593-1633)

It is indeed right, our duty and our joy,
always and everywhere to give you thanks,
Almighty and eternal Father,
and in these days of Easter
to celebrate with joyful hearts
the memory of your wonderful works.

For by the mystery of his passion
Jesus Christ, your risen Son,
has conquered the powers of death and hell
and restored in us the image of his glory
to place us once more in paradise
and open to us the gate of life eternal.

And so, in the joy of this Passover,
earth and heaven resound with gladness,
while angels and archangels and the powers of all creation
for ever sing the hymn of your eternal glory.

From the Ambrosian Preface for the second Wednesday of Easter

Easter Day

Christ our Passover has been sacrificed for us: therefore let us keep the feast with the unleavened bread of sincerity and truth.

1 Corinthians 5.7–8

For reflection

This is the day that the Lord has made:
Let us rejoice and be glad in it. Alleluia!

Collect Lord of all life and power,
who through the mighty resurrection of your Son
overcame the old order of sin and death
to make all things new in him:
grant that we, being dead to sin and alive to you in Jesus Christ,
may reign with him in glory;
to whom with you and the Holy Spirit
be praise and honour, glory and might,
now and in all eternity.

Ascension

The Ascension, historicized by Luke as the final parting from his disciples by the risen Christ, has great significance for our discipleship today. First, there is Jesus' promise to his disciples that his return to the Father was a necessary prelude to the outpouring of the Holy Spirit: no longer would the presence of God with his people be limited to the particularity of one person at one time and in one place.

I will not leave you desolate ... The Counsellor, the Holy Spirit, whom the Father will send in my name, will teach you all things. It is to your advantage that I go away, for if I do not go away, the Counsellor will not come to you; but if I go, I will send him to you.

John 14.18,26 and 16.7

Among the images of a royal coronation are those derived from those psalms that celebrate the bringing of the ark up to Jerusalem and enthroning it in the Temple.

> God has gone up with a merry noise:
> And the Lord with the sound of a trumpet.

Psalm 47.5

There are those that speak of the transformation of the dying king on the cross into the triumphant Lord of all the world:

> The head that once was crowned with thorns
>   Is crowned with glory now:
> A royal diadem adorns
>   The mighty victor's brow.

And most significant are those which claim that in Christ's Ascension to the Father we too are given a place at the right hand of God. This is how the writer of the Letter to the Hebrews sees Christ bringing our prayer before the Father's throne eternally.

> Thou hast raised our human nature
>   In the clouds to God's right hand;
> There we sit in heavenly places,
>   There with thee in glory stand;
> Jesus reigns, adored by angels;
>   Man with God is on the throne;
> Mighty Lord, in thine Ascension
>   We by faith behold our own.

Christopher Wordsworth (1807-1885)

Jesus has gone as a forerunner on our behalf, having become a high priest for ever after the order of Melchizedek ... He holds his priesthood permanently, because he continues for ever. Consequently he is able for all time to save those who draw near to God through him since he ever lives to make intercession for us.

God is gone up with a triumphant shout:
The Lord with sounding trumpet's melodies:
Sing Praise, sing praises out,
Unto our King sing praises seraphicwise!
And let the King of glory enter in.

Methinks I see Heaven's sparkling courtiers fly,
In flakes of glory down him to attend,
And hear heart-cramping notes of melody
Surround his chariot as it did ascend,
Mixing their music, making every string
More to enravish as they this tune sing.

God is gone up with a triumphant shout:
The Lord with sounding trumpet's melodies:
Sing Praise, sing praises out,
Unto our King sing praises seraphicwise!
And let the King of glory enter in.

Edward Taylor (1646-1729)

Why do you stand looking up toward heaven? This Jesus, who has
been taken up from you into heaven, will come in the same way as you
saw him go into heaven.

Acts 1.11

For reflection

I am ascending to my Father and to your Father,
To my God and your God. Alleluia!

Collect Grant, we pray, almighty God,
that as we believe your only-begotten Son our Lord Jesus Christ
to have ascended into the heavens,
so we in heart and mind may also ascend
and with him continually dwell;
who is alive and reigns with you in the unity of the Holy Spirit,
one God, now and for ever.

Pentecost

The fiftieth day of Easter brings the season to a close with the celebration that marks the moment when the disciples had tumbled to it that the power of the risen life had indeed been handed over to them: they were the witnesses of the risen Christ; they were to be the agent of God's love; they were to be lights in the world. This great outward movement of the followers of Christ was matched by a great outpouring of energy, and the celebration of Pentecost is full of fire and wind, energy and life.

The dove descending breaks the air
With flame of incandescent terror
Of which the tongues declare
The one discharge from sin and error.
The only hope, or else despair
   Lies in the choice of pyre or pyre —
   To be redeemed from fire by fire.

Who then devised the torment? Love.
Love is the unfamiliar Name
Behind the hands that wove
The intolerable shirt of flame
Which human power cannot remove.
   We only live, only suspire
   Consumed by either fire or fire.

T. S. Eliot (1888-1965), an extract from 'Little Gidding'

Listen sweet Dove unto my song,
And spread thy golden wings in me;
Hatching my tender heart so long
Till it get wing, and flie away with thee.

Where is that fire which once descended
On thy Apostles? thou didst then
Keep open house, richly attended,
Feasting all comers by twelve chosen men.

Such glorious gifts thou didst bestow,
That th'earth did like a heav'n appeare;
The starres were coming down to know
If they might mend their wages, and serve here.

The sunne, which once did shine alone,
Hung down his head, and wisht for night,
When he beheld twelve sunnes for one
Going about the world, and giving light.

But since those pipes of gold, which brought
That cordiall water to our ground,
Were cut and martyr'd by the fault
Of those, who did themselves through their side wound

Thou shutt'st the doore, and keep'st within;
Scarce a good joy creeps through the chink;
And if the braves of conquering sinne
Did not excite thee, we should wholly sink.

Lord, though we change, thou art the same;
The same sweet God of love and light:
Restore this day, for thy great name,
Unto his ancient and miraculous right.

George Herbert (1593-1633)

Unless the eye catch fire
    The God will not be seen.
Unless the ear catch fire
    The God will not be heard.
Unless the tongue catch fire
    The God will not be named.
Unless the heart catch fire
    The God will not be loved.
Unless the mind catch fire
    The God will not be known.

William Blake (1757-1827), an extract from 'Pentecost'

Jesus said, 'I will ask the Father and he will give you another advocate, to be with you for ever, the Spirit of truth.'

John 14.16—17a

For reflection

The Spirit of the Lord fills the whole earth. Alleluia!

The Spirit searches all things, even the depths of God. Alleluia!

The Spirit of the Lord enables us to cry out, 'Abba, Father!'

Come, Holy Spirit, fill the hearts of your faithful people
and kindle in us the fire of your love. Alleluia!

Collect God, who as at this time
    taught the hearts of your faithful people
    by sending to them the light of your Holy Spirit:
    grant us by the same Spirit
    to have a right judgement in all things
    and evermore to rejoice in his holy comfort;
    through the merits of Christ Jesus our Saviour,
    who is alive and reigns with you,
    in the unity of the Holy Spirit,
    one God, now and for ever.

Trinity Sunday

In Orthodox iconography, the Holy Trinity is represented by the three angels who came to visit Abraham, bringing the news that the elderly Abraham and Sarah will have a son. They sit round a table, their wings touching, holding their tall messenger's rods, as they wait for Abraham's meal. The most frequently reproduced icon, by Andrei Rublev, almost seems to incorporate the viewer as the fourth person at the table, representing the way in which we are enfolded into the communion of the divine life of the Holy Trinity. The Feast of the Holy Trinity was a particularly English observance, as is the tradition of naming the Sundays of 'Ordinary Time' — the green Sundays — Sundays after Trinity.

St Patrick's Breastplate

> I bind unto myself today
> The strong name of the Trinity,
> By invocation of the same,
> The Three in One, and One in Three.
>
> I bind this day to me for ever,
> By power of faith, Christ's Incarnation;
> His baptism in Jordan river;
> His death on Cross for my salvation;
> His bursting from the spiced tomb;
> His riding up the heavenly way;
> His coming at the day of doom;
> I bind unto myself today.
>
> I bind unto myself the power
> Of the great love of Cherubim;
> The sweet 'Well done' in judgement hour;
> The service of the Seraphim,
> Confessors' faith, Apostles' word,
> The Patriarchs' prayers, the Prophets' scrolls,
> All good deeds done unto the Lord,
> And purity of virgin souls.

I bind unto myself today
The virtues of the star-lit heaven,
The glorious sun's life-giving ray,
The whiteness of the moon at even,
The flashing of the lightning free,
The whirling wind's tempestuous shocks,
The stable earth, the deep salt sea,
Around the old eternal rocks.

I bind unto myself today
The power of God to hold and lead,
His eye to watch, his might to stay,
His ear to hearken to my need.
The wisdom of my God to teach,
His hand to guide, his shield to ward;
The word of God to give me speech,
His heavenly host to be my guard.

Christ be with me, Christ within me,
Christ behind me, Christ before me,
Christ beside me, Christ to win me,
Christ to comfort and restore me.
Christ beneath me, Christ above me,
Christ in quiet, Christ in danger,
Christ in hearts of all who love me,
Christ in mouth of friend and stranger.

I bind unto myself the name,
The strong name of the Trinity;
By invocation of the same,
The Three in One, and One in Three.
Of whom all nature hath creation;
Eternal Father, Spirit, Word:
Praise to the Lord of my salvation,
Salvation is of Christ the Lord.

St Patrick (372-466), tr. Mrs C. F. Alexander (1818-1895)

Glimpses of the divine:

The Bright Field

> I have seen the sun break through
> to illuminate a small field
> for a while, and gone my way
> and forgotten it. But that was the pearl
> of great price, the one field that had
> the treasure in it. I realize now
> that I must give all that I have
> to possess it. Life is not hurrying
>
> on to a receding future, nor hankering after
> an imagined past. It is the turning
> aside like Moses to the miracle
> of the lit bush, to a brightness
> that seemed as transitory as your youth
> once, but is the eternity that awaits you.

R. S. Thomas (1913-2001)

Jesus said to the disciples, 'Go, therefore, and make disciples of all nations, baptizing them in the name of the Father and of the Son and of the Holy Spirit.'

Matthew 28.19

For reflection

> Holy, holy, holy is the Lord of hosts,
> Who was, and is, and who is to come.

Collect Almighty and everlasting God,
> you have given us your servants grace,
> by the confession of a true faith,
> to acknowledge the glory of the eternal Trinity
> and in the power of the divine majesty to worship the Unity:
> keep us steadfast in this faith,
> that we may evermore be defended from all adversities;
> through Jesus Christ our Lord.

Corpus Christi (Thursday after Trinity Sunday)

The day of thanksgiving for the institution of Holy Communion. Corpus Christi provides an opportunity for thanking God for the gift of Jesus' real presence in our midst in the Eucharist, and for the reminder of his continuing presence with us. The celebration complements that of Maundy Thursday, where the focus shifts so quickly from the Upper Room to the Agony in the Garden. You may also like to use the Eucharistic Devotions on pp.111-112.

> Jesus said, 'I am the bread of life. Whoever eats my flesh and drinks my blood has eternal life, and I will raise them up at the last day. Those who eat my flesh and drink my blood abide in me and I in them.'

John 6.35a,54,56

For reflection
> Mortals ate the food of angels,
> for you gave them bread from heaven.

Collect Lord Jesus Christ,
> we thank you that in this wonderful sacrament
> you have given us the memorial of your passion:
> grant us so to reverence the sacred mysteries
> of your body and blood
> that we may know within ourselves
> and show forth in our lives the fruits of your redemption;
> for you are alive and reign, now and for ever.

5.3 The Christian Year: Festivals and Saints' Days

Prologue

From the account of the Martyrdom of Polycarp

As Polycarp was entering the stadium, there came a voice to him from heaven, *Be strong, Polycarp, and play the man.* The speaker indeed no one saw, but the voice was heard by those of our friends who were present. Then he was brought forward, and great was the din as they heard that Polycarp was arrested. So he was brought before the Proconsul, who asked him if he were Polycarp? He said 'Yes,' and the Proconsul tried to persuade him to deny his faith, urging... 'Swear, and I release you; curse Christ.' And Polycarp said, 'Eighty-six years have I served Him, and He has done me no wrong: how then can I blaspheme my King who saved me?'

The Proconsul said, 'I have wild beasts; if you will not change your mind I will throw you to them.' Then he said, 'Bid them be brought: change of mind from better to worse is not a change that we are allowed; but to change from wrong to right is good.' Then again said the Proconsul to him, 'If you despise the beasts, unless you change your mind, I shall have you burnt ...'

Forthwith then all the gear adapted for the pyre was put about him. They were on the point of fastening him with nails, but he said, 'Let me be as I am: He that gives me power to abide the fire will grant me too without your making me fast with nails to stay at the pyre unflinching.'

So they did not nail him, but they bound him. He put his hands behind him and was bound, like a goodly ram out of a great flock for an offering, a whole burnt offering made ready and acceptable to God. Then he looked up to heaven and said,

O Lord God Almighty, Father of Thy beloved and blessed child Jesus Christ, through whom we have received our knowledge of Thee, God of Angels and Powers and of all creation and of the whole race of the righteous who live before Thy face, I bless Thee in that Thou hast deemed me worthy of this day and hour; that I might take a portion among the martyrs in the cup of Christ, to the resurrection of eternal life both of soul and body in the incorruption of the Holy Ghost. Among these may I today be welcome before thy face as a rich and acceptable sacrifice as thou didst prepare and manifest beforehand and didst fulfil, thou the faithful and true God. For this cause and for all things I praise thee, I bless thee, I glorify thee through the everlasting and heavenly high priest Jesus Christ thy beloved Son, through whom to thee with him and the Holy Spirit be glory now and for the ages to come. Amen.

When he had offered up his Amen and completed his prayer, those in charge kindled the fire. A great flame flashed out, and we to whom the sight was granted, saw a marvel; and we moreover were preserved to the end that we might tell to the rest what came to pass. The fire made the appearance of a vaulted roof, like a ship's sail filling out with the wind, and it walled about the body of the martyr in a ring. There was it in the midst, not like flesh burning, but like a loaf baking, or like gold and silver being refined in a furnace. Moreover we caught a fragrance as of the breath of frankincense or some other precious spice.

In the end, when the lawless mob had seen that his body could not be consumed by the fire they commanded an executioner to go and stab him with a dagger. He did this and there came out so much blood that it put out the fire, and all the multitude marvelled at the mighty difference between the unbelievers and the elect, of whom one was this man, the most admirable Polycarp, who in our times was an apostolic and prophetic teacher, bishop of the Holy Church in Smyrna.

God grant us to be made sharers alike of his lot and of his discipleship.

The Conception of the Blessed Virgin Mary (8 December)

The Lord himself will give you a sign: look, the virgin is with child
and shall bear a son, and shall name him Emmanuel, God is with us.

Isaiah 7.14

For reflection

The Almighty has done great things for me
and holy is his name!

Collect Almighty and everlasting God,
who stooped to raise fallen humanity
through the child-bearing of blessèd Mary:
grant that we, who have seen your glory
revealed in our human nature
and your love made perfect in our weakness,
may daily be renewed in your image
and conformed to the pattern of your Son
Jesus Christ our Lord.

Stephen the First Martyr (26 December)

As they were stoning Stephen, he prayed, 'Lord Jesus, receive my
spirit.' And he knelt down and cried with a loud voice, 'Lord, do not
hold this sin against them.' And when he had said this, he fell asleep.

Acts 8.59–60

Collect Gracious Father, who gave the first martyr Stephen
grace to pray for those who took up stones against him:
grant that in all our sufferings for the truth
we may learn to love even our enemies
and to seek forgiveness for those who desire our hurt,
looking up to heaven to him who was crucified for us,
Jesus Christ, our mediator and advocate.

John the Evangelist (27 December)

Collect   Merciful Lord,
cast your bright beams of light upon the Church:
that, being enlightened by the teaching
of your blessèd apostle and evangelist Saint John,
we may so walk in the light of your truth
that we may at last attain to the light of everlasting life;
through Jesus Christ your incarnate Son our Lord.

The Holy Innocents (28 December)

Collect   Heavenly Father,
whose children suffered at the hands of Herod,
though they had done no wrong:
by the suffering of your Son and by the innocence of our lives
frustrate all evil designs
and establish your reign of justice and peace;
through Jesus Christ our Lord.

New Year's Eve (31 December)

In the beginning, Lord, you founded the earth, and the heavens
are the work of your hands; they will perish but you remain;
they will all grow old like a garment, like a cloak you will roll
them up, and they will be changed. But you are the same, and
your years will never end.

Hebrews 1.10–12

Collect   God and Father of our Lord Jesus Christ, whose years never fail
and whose mercies are new each returning day:
let the radiance of your Spirit renew our lives,
warming our hearts and giving light to our minds;
that we may pass the coming year
in joyful obedience and firm faith;
through him who is the beginning and the end,
your Son Jesus Christ our Lord.

The Naming and Circumcision of Jesus (1 January)

> Peter, filled with the Holy Spirit, said, 'Be it known to you all that by
> the name of Jesus of Nazareth, whom you crucified, whom God
> raised from the dead, by him this man is standing before you well.
> There is salvation in no one else, for there is no other name under
> heaven given among mortals by which we must be saved.'
>
> *Acts 4.10,12*

For reflection

> At the name of Jesus
> every knee shall bow.

Collect Almighty God, whose blessèd Son was circumcised
in obedience to the law for our sake
and given the Name that is above every name:
give us grace faithfully to bear his Name,
to worship him in the freedom of the Spirit,
and to proclaim him as the Saviour of the world.

The Conversion of St Paul (25 January)

*The celebration of St Paul's Conversion marks the end of the Week of Prayer for
Christian Unity (see Chapter 6.8 on p.213f.). The account of Paul's conversion,
read at the Eucharist, is from the Acts of the Apostles 9.1–19.*

> For I want you to know that the gospel that was proclaimed by me is
> not of human origin; for I did not receive it from a human source, nor
> was I taught it, but I received it through a revelation of Jesus Christ.
>
> *Galatians 1.11–12*

For reflection

> Faith comes by hearing
> and hearing by the word of Christ.

Collect Almighty God,
who caused the light of the gospel to shine throughout the world
through the preaching of your servant Saint Paul:
grant that we who celebrate his wonderful conversion
may follow him in bearing witness to your truth;
through Jesus Christ our Lord.

Joseph, Husband of the Blessed Virgin Mary (19 March)

Collect God our Father,
who from the family of your servant David
raised up Joseph the carpenter
to be the guardian of your incarnate Son
and husband of the Blessèd Virgin Mary:
give us grace to follow him
in faithful obedience to your commands;
through Jesus Christ our Lord.

The Annunciation of Our Lord to the Blessed Virgin Mary (25 March)

The angel said, 'The Holy Spirit will come upon you, Mary, and the power of the Most High will overshadow you; therefore the child to be born will be holy, and will be called the Son of God.'

Luke 1.35

For reflection
Behold, the handmaid of the Lord;
let it be to me according to your word.

Collect We beseech you, O Lord,
pour your grace into our hearts,
that as we have known the incarnation of your Son Jesus Christ
by the message of an angel,
so by his cross and passion
we may be brought to the glory of his resurrection;
through Jesus Christ our Lord.

George, Martyr, Patron of England (23 April)

Collect God of hosts,
who so kindled the flame of love
in the heart of your servant George
that he bore witness to the risen Lord
by his life and by his death:
give us the same faith and power of love
that we who rejoice in his triumphs
may come to share with him the fullness of the resurrection;
through Jesus Christ your Son our Lord.

Mark, Evangelist (25 April)

Collect Almighty God,
who enlightened your holy Church
through the inspired witness of your evangelist Saint Mark:
grant that we, being firmly grounded
in the truth of the gospel,
may be faithful to its teaching both in word and deed;
through Jesus Christ your Son our Lord.

Philip and James, Apostles (1 May)

Collect Almighty Father,
whom truly to know is eternal life:
teach us to know your Son Jesus Christ
as the way, the truth, and the life;
that we may follow the steps
of your holy apostles Philip and James,
and walk steadfastly in the way that leads to your glory;
through Jesus Christ your Son our Lord.

Matthias, Apostle (14 May)

Collect Almighty God,
who in the place of the traitor Judas
chose your faithful servant Matthias
to be of the number of the Twelve:
preserve your Church from false apostles
and, by the ministry of faithful pastors and teachers,
keep us steadfast in your truth;
through Jesus Christ your Son our Lord.

The Visit of the Blessed Virgin Mary to Elizabeth (31 May)

Elizabeth heard Mary's greeting and her child leapt in her
womb. Elizabeth exclaimed with a loud cry: 'Blessèd are you
among women, and blessèd is the fruit of your womb.'

Luke 1.41,42

For reflection
God has looked with favour on his lowly servant;
from this day, all generations shall call her blessèd.

Collect Mighty God,
by whose grace Elizabeth rejoiced with Mary
and greeted her as the mother of the Lord:
look with favour on your lowly servants
that, with Mary, we may magnify your holy name
and rejoice to acclaim her Son our Saviour Jesus Christ.

Barnabas, Apostle (11 June)

Collect Bountiful God, giver of all gifts,
who poured your Spirit upon your servant Barnabas
and gave him grace to encourage others:
help us, by his example,
to be generous in our judgements
and unselfish in our service;
through Jesus Christ your Son our Lord.

The Birth of John the Baptist (24 June)

'Truly I tell you,' said Jesus, 'among those born of women, no
one has arisen greater than John the Baptist.'

Matthew 11.11

For reflection

See, I am sending my messenger ahead of me,
to prepare my way before me.

Collect Almighty God,
by whose providence your servant John the Baptist
was wonderfully born,
and sent to prepare the way of your Son our Saviour
by the preaching of repentance:
lead us to repent according to his preaching
and, after his example,
constantly to speak the truth, boldly to rebuke vice,
and patiently to suffer for the truth's sake;
through Jesus Christ our Lord.

Peter and Paul Apostles (29 June)

God, who worked through Peter, making him an apostle to the
circumcised, also worked through me, in sending me to the Gentiles.

Galatians 2.8

For reflection

Their voice has gone out to all the earth
and their words to the ends of the world.

Collect Almighty God,
whose blessèd apostles Peter and Paul
glorified you in their death as in their life:
grant that your Church,
inspired by their teaching and example,
and made one by your Spirit,
may ever stand firm upon the one foundation,
Jesus Christ your Son our Lord.

Thomas, Apostle (3 July)

Collect Almighty and eternal God,
who, for the firmer foundation of our faith,
allowed your holy apostle Thomas
to doubt the resurrection of your Son
till word and sight convinced him:
grant to us, who have not seen, that we also may believe
and so confess Christ as our Lord and our God.

Mary Magdalene, Apostle to the Apostles (22 July)

Jesus said to Mary, 'Woman, why are you weeping? For whom are you looking?' Supposing him to be the gardener, she said to him, 'Sir, if you have carried him away, tell me where you have laid him, and I will take him away.' Jesus said to her, 'Mary!' She turned and said to him in Hebrew, 'Rabbouni!', which means Teacher.

John 20.15–16

For reflection
Mary came and told the disciples:
I have seen the Lord.

Collect Almighty God,
whose Son restored Mary Magdalene to health of mind and body
and called her to be a witness to his resurrection:
forgive our sins and heal us by your grace,
that we may serve you in the power of his risen life;
who is alive and reigns with you in the unity of the Holy Spirit,
one God, now and for ever.

James, Apostle (25 July)

Collect Merciful God,
whose holy apostle Saint James,
leaving his father and all that he had,
was obedient to the calling of your Son Jesus Christ
and followed him even to death:
help us, forsaking the false attractions of the world,
to be ready at all times to answer your call without delay;
through Jesus Christ your Son our Lord.

The Transfiguration of Our Lord (6 August)

> Jesus said, 'Father, glorify your name.' Then a voice came from
> heaven, 'I have glorified it and I will glorify it again.'
>
> *John 12.28*

For reflection
> It is good that we are here
> to behold the glory that is Christ.

Collect Father in heaven,
> whose Son Jesus Christ was wonderfully transfigured
> before chosen witnesses upon the holy mountain,
> and spoke of the exodus he would accomplish at Jerusalem:
> give us strength so to hear his voice and bear our cross
> that in the world to come we may see him as he is;
> who is alive and reigns with you in the unity of the Holy Spirit,
> one God, now and for ever.

The Blessed Virgin Mary (15 August)

Collect Almighty God,
> who looked upon the lowliness of the blessèd Virgin Mary
> and chose her to be the mother of your only Son:
> grant that we who are redeemed by his blood
> may share with her in the glory of your eternal kingdom;
> through Jesus Christ our Lord.

Bartholomew, Apostle (24 August)

Collect Almighty and everlasting God,
> who gave to your apostle Bartholomew grace
> truly to believe and to preach your word:
> grant that your Church
> may love that word which he believed
> and may faithfully preach and receive the same;
> through Jesus Christ your Son our Lord.

Nativity of the Blessed Virgin Mary (8 September)

When the time had fully come, God sent forth his Son, born of a
woman, born under the law, to redeem those who were under the law,
so that we might receive adoption as children.

Galatians 4.4–5

For reflection

Blessèd are you, O Virgin Mary, for you believed
that what was said to you by the Lord would be fulfilled.

Collect Almighty and everlasting God,
who stooped to raise fallen humanity
through the child-bearing of blessèd Mary:
grant that we, who have seen your glory
revealed in our human nature
and your love made perfect in our weakness,
may daily be renewed in your image
and conformed to the pattern of your Son,
Jesus Christ our Lord.

Holy Cross Day (14 September)

Christ abolished the law with its commandments and ordinances,
that he might create in himself one new humanity in place of the two,
thus making peace, and might reconcile both to God in one body
through the cross.

Ephesians 2.15–16

For reflection

Far be it from me to glory
save in the cross of our Lord Jesus Christ.

Collect Almighty God,
who in the passion of your blessèd Son
made an instrument of painful death
to be for us the means of life and peace:
grant us so to glory in the cross of Christ
that we may gladly suffer for his sake;
who is alive and reigns with you in the unity of the Holy Spirit,
one God, now and for ever.

Matthew, Apostle (21 September)

Collect O Almighty God,
  whose blessed Son called Matthew the tax collector
  to be an apostle and evangelist:
  give us grace to forsake the selfish pursuit of gain
  and the possessive love of riches
  that we may follow in the way of your Son Jesus Christ.

Michael and All Angels (29 September)

  Jesus said, 'Truly, I say to you, you will see heaven opened, and the
  angels of God ascending and descending upon the Son of man.'

  John 1.51

For reflection
  The Lord commanded his angels
  to keep you in all your ways.

Collect Everlasting God,
  you have ordained and constituted
  the ministries of angels and mortals in a wonderful order:
  grant that as your holy angels always serve you in heaven,
  so, at your command, they may help and defend us on earth;
  through Jesus Christ our Lord.

Luke, Evangelist (18 October)

Collect Almighty God,
  you called Luke the physician,
  whose praise is in the gospel,
  to be an evangelist and physician of the soul:
  by the grace of the Spirit
  and through the wholesome medicine of the gospel,
  give your Church the same love and power to heal;
  through Jesus Christ your Son our Lord.

Simon and Jude, Apostles (28 October)

Collect Almighty God,
who built your Church upon the foundation
of the apostles and prophets,
with Jesus Christ himself as the chief cornerstone:
so join us together in unity of spirit by their doctrine,
that we may be made a holy temple acceptable to you;
through Jesus Christ your Son our Lord,
who is alive and reigns with you,
in the unity of the Holy Spirit,
one God, now and for ever.

All Saints' Day (1 November)

There was a great multitude, which no one could number, from
every nation, from all tribes and peoples and languages, standing
before the throne and before the Lamb, robed in white, with
palm branches in their hands. They cried out in a loud voice saying:
'Salvation belongs to our God, who is seated on the throne,
and to the Lamb!'

Revelation 7.9–10

For Reflection
The righteous will shine like the sun
in the kingdom of the Father.

Collect Almighty God, you have knit together your elect
in one communion and fellowship
in the mystical body of your Son Christ our Lord:
grant us grace so to follow your blessèd saints
in all virtuous and godly living
that we may come to those inexpressible joys
that you have prepared for those who truly love you;
through Jesus Christ our Lord.

All Souls' Day (2 November)

> The souls of the righteous are in the hand of God
> and no torment will ever touch them.
> In the eyes of the foolish, they seem to have died;
> but they are at peace.
> For though, in the sight of others, they were punished,
> their hope is full of immortality.
> Having been disciplined a little,
> they will receive great good,
> because God tested them and found them worthy.
> Like gold in the furnace, God tried them
> and, like a sacrificial burnt offering, accepted them.
> In the time of their visitation, they will shine forth
> and will run like sparks through the stubble.
> They will govern nations and rule over peoples
> and God will reign over them for ever.

Wisdom 3.1,2a,3b–8

For reflection

> I am the resurrection and the life;
> whoever believes in me, though they die, yet shall they live.

Collect Eternal God, our maker and redeemer,
grant us, with all the faithful departed,
the sure benefits of your Son's saving passion and glorious resurrection
that, in the last day, when you gather up all things in Christ,
we may with them enjoy the fullness of your promises;
through Jesus Christ our Lord.

Andrew, Apostle (30 November)

Collect Almighty God,
who gave such grace to your apostle Saint Andrew
that he readily obeyed the call of your Son Jesus Christ
and brought his brother with him:
call us by your holy word,
and give us grace to follow you without delay
and to tell the good news of your kingdom;
through Jesus Christ your Son our Lord.

Christl the King (Sunday next before Advent)

God raised Christ from the dead and enthroned him at his right
hand in the heavenly realms, far above all government and
authority, all power and dominion.

Ephesians 1.20—21

For reflection

God raised Christ from the dead
and enthroned him at his right hand in heaven.

Collect Eternal Father,
whose Son Jesus Christ ascended to the throne of heaven
that he might rule over all things as Lord and King:
keep the Church in the unity of the Spirit
and in the bond of peace,
and bring the whole created order to worship at his feet;
who is alive and reigns, now and for ever.

5.4 The Blessed Virgin Mary

Her Virgin eyes saw God incarnate born,
When she to Bethlehem came that happy morn;
How high her raptures then began to swell,
None but her own omniscient Son can tell.

As Eve, when she her fontal sin reviewed,
Wept for herself and all she should include,
Blest Mary with man's Saviour in embrace
Joyed for herself and all the human race.

All saints are by her Son's dear influence blest;
She kept the very fountain at her breast;
The Son adored and nursed by the sweet maid
A thousandfold of love for love repaid.

Heaven with transcendent joys her entrance graced;
Next to his throne her Son his Mother placed;
And here below, now she's of heaven possest,
All generations are to call her blest.

Thomas Ken (1637-1711)

Anthem to the Theotokos

Into his joy, the Lord has received you,
Virgin God-bearer, Mother of Christ.

You have beheld the King in his beauty,
Mary, daughter of Israel.

You have made answer for the creation
To the redeeming will of God.

Light, fire and life, divine and immortal,
Joined to our nature you have brought forth,

That to the glory of God the Father,
Heaven and earth might be restored.

Greek Orthodox Hymn, tr. by West Malling Abbey

Salve Regina – an Anthem Before Sleep

Traditionally, this anthem is sung at the end of Night Prayer from after Pentecost to Advent.

Salve, Regina, mater misericordiae;
Hail, O Queen, mother of mercy;
vita, dulcedo, et spes nostra, salve.
our life, our sweetness and our hope, hail.
Ad te clamamus, exsules, filii Evae,
To you do we cry, the banished, children of Eve;
ad te suspiramus,
to you do we sigh,
gementes et flentes in hac lacrimarum valle;
lamenting and weeping in this vale of tears;
eia, ergo, advocata nostra,
therefore, our advocate,
illos tuos misericordes oculos ad nos converte,
your eyes of mercy turn towards us,
Et Iesum, benedictum fructum ventris tui,
And Jesus, the blessèd fruit of your womb,
nobis post hoc exsilium ostende,
to us, after this exile, reveal,
O clemens, O pia, O dulcis Virgo Maria.
O clement, O devoted, O sweet Virgin Mary.

The Angelic Salutation (The Angelus)

Traditionally said at morning, noon and nightfall. The 'Hail Mary' is a common refrain among other prayers, for example in saying the Rosary.

The Angel of the Lord brought tidings to Mary
and she conceived by the Holy Spirit.

Hail Mary, full of grace, the Lord is with you.
Blessèd are you among women,
and blessèd is the fruit of your womb, Jesus.
Holy Mary, Mother of God, pray for us sinners,
now, and at the hour of our death. Amen.

'Behold, the handmaid of the Lord;
let it be to me according to your word.'

Hail Mary, full of grace, the Lord is with you.
Blessèd are you among women,
and blessèd is the fruit of your womb, Jesus.
Holy Mary, Mother of God, pray for us sinners,
now, and at the hour of our death. Amen.

The Word was made flesh
and dwelt among us.

Hail Mary, full of grace, the Lord is with you.
Blessèd are you among women,
and blessèd is the fruit of your womb, Jesus.
Holy Mary, Mother of God, pray for us sinners,
now, and at the hour of our death. Amen.

Pray for us, O holy Mother of God,
that we may be made worthy of the promises of Christ.

Let us pray

We beseech you, O Lord,
to pour your grace into our hearts;
that as we have known the incarnation
of your Son Jesus Christ
by the message of an angel,
so by his ✠ cross and passion
we may be brought to the glory of his resurrection;
through Jesus Christ our Lord. Amen.

The Rosary

Many religions have a tradition of using patterns or counting devices to absorb the body while the spirit freewheels. A solitaire board was found in the grave of an early nun in Egypt, and people have used an abacus; but the traditional Rosary is a knotted cord or a string of beads. If you have one, you may like to try using it. The idea is to move your finger over the beads as you say prayers you know by heart while in your mind you hold one of the 'mysteries', as some of the traditional themes for meditation are called.

On a traditional rosary there are five groups of ten beads, each separated by a single bead, or one of a different colour. From the bottom hangs a tail, with one then three then one bead, and finally a crucifix. Holding the crucifix, you say the Apostles' Creed; on the first bead you say the Our Father, then the Hail Mary on the next three as you think about the work of Father, the Son and the Holy Spirit, and the Glory be on the last. As you move round the five groups of ten, you say the Our Father on the bead that separates each one, and the Hail Mary on each of the ten.

The traditional themes for meditation are

The Five Joyful Mysteries
The Annunciation of the Angel to Mary	*Luke 1.26–38*
The Visitation of Mary to Elizabeth	*Luke 1.39–56*
The Nativity of our Lord	*Luke 2.1–10*
The Presentation in the Temple	*Luke 2.22–38*
Finding Jesus among the Doctors in the Temple	*Luke 2.41–52*

The Five Sorrowful Mysteries
The Agony in the Garden	*Luke 22.39–46*
The Scourging at the Pillar	*Matthew 27.11–26*
The Crowning with Thorns	*Matthew 27.26–31*
The Carrying of the Cross	*Luke 23.26–32*
The Crucifixion and Death of our Lord	*Luke 23.32–47*

The Five Glorious Mysteries
The Resurrection	*Luke 24.13–35*
The Ascension	*Acts 1.1–11*
The Coming of the Holy Spirit on the Church	*Acts 2.1–13*
The Assumption of our Lady	*cf. Luke 1.42–50*
The Coronation of our Lady	*Revelation 12.1–6*

If you are helped by this pattern of praying, you may like to vary it, either by substituting the Jesus Prayer for the Hail Mary, or by composing other Mysteries from the life and teachings of our Lord, or the saints. Pope John Paul II has recently added another, asking that it be prayed especially on Sundays.

The Five Mysteries of Light

Christ's Baptism in the Jordan	*Mark 1.1–10*
Christ's self-revelation at the first miracle in Cana	*John 2.1–11*
Christ's announcement of the Kingdom of God, with the invitation to conversion	*Matthew 4.12–22*
Christ's Transfiguration, when he revealed his glory to the Apostles	*Mark 9.2–8*
The institution of the Eucharist at the Last Supper	*Mark 14.12–26*

6 Sacramental Themes

6.1 Remembering Baptism

Baptism is the keystone of our faith. A spring, a flowing stream or waterfall, even a bowl of water or the bath on Saturday evening before Sunday morning may remind you of your dying to sin and rising to start a new life in Christ.

God in Christ gives us water welling up for eternal life.
With joy you will draw water from the wells of salvation.

With you is the well of life
and in your light shall we see light.

Lord, give us this water and we shall thirst no more.

Thus says the Lord who created you, O Jacob, he who formed
you, O Israel: Fear not, for I have redeemed you; I have called
you by name, you are mine. When you pass through the waters,
I will be with you; and through the rivers, they shall not overwhelm
you; when you walk through fire, you shall not be
burned and the flame shall not consume you. For I am the Lord
your God, the Holy One of Israel, your Saviour.

Isaiah 43.1–3a

Jesus came from Nazareth of Galilee and was baptized by John
in the Jordan. And just as he was coming up out of the water, he
saw the heavens torn apart and the Spirit descending like a dove
on him. And a voice came from heaven, 'You are my Son, the
Belovèd; with you I am well pleased.'

Mark 1.9–11

In early days, new Christians completed their preparation during Lent, and were baptized, anointed with Chrism and joined in celebrating the Eucharist together for the first time at the all-night Easter Liturgy. In the weeks after Easter, the bishop recalled what had happened to them and helped them think through their new responsibilities. Cyril of Jerusalem asks the newly baptized to think back to the moment of their baptism.

When you went down into the water, it was like the night,
and you could see nothing. But when you came up again
it was like finding yourself in the day. That one moment
was your death and your birth; that saving water was
both your grave and your mother.

Mystagogical Catecheses II.4

St Paul connects our baptism with the death and resurrection of Christ:

Do you not know that all of us who have been baptized into
Christ Jesus were baptized into his death? Therefore we have
been buried with him by baptism into death so that, as Christ
was raised from the dead by the glory of the Father, we too
might walk in newness of life.

Romans 6.3—4

The Eastern tradition stresses baptism as a new birth, the first step along the road to a new life in Christ, as St John's Gospel proclaims:

Jesus said, 'Truly, truly I say to you, unless one is born anew,
he cannot see the kingdom of God.' Nicodemus said to him,
'How can a man be born when he is old? Can he enter a second
time into his mother's womb and be born?' Jesus answered,
'Truly, truly I say to you, unless one is born of water and the Spirit,
he cannot enter the kingdom of God.'

John 3.3—5

Blessèd are you, Sovereign God of all,
you are our light and our salvation.
From the deep waters of death
you have raised your Son to life in triumph.
May we, with all who have been born anew
by water and the Spirit,
be renewed in your image,
walk by the light of faith,
and serve you in newness of life;
through your anointed Son, Jesus Christ,
to whom with you and the Holy Spirit
we lift our voices of praise:
Blessèd be God for ever.

As you recall your baptism, you may like to sign yourself with the cross, saying:

✠ In the name of the Father,
and of the Son,
and of the Holy Spirit. Amen

Or you may like to use the Apostles' Creed that has been used at baptism since the earliest days of the Church. See p.4.

May God, who has received me by baptism into his church
pour upon me the riches of his grace,
that within the company of Christ's pilgrim people
I may daily be renewed by his anointing Spirit
until I come to the inheritance of the saints in glory.

As you recall your Confirmation, pray:

Defend, O Lord, your servant with your heavenly grace,
that I may continue yours for ever,
and daily increase in your holy Spirit more and more,
until I come to your everlasting kingdom.

The blessing

May God, who in Christ gives us a spring of water
welling up to eternal life,
perfect in us the image of his glory;
and may God almighty bless us,
Father, the Son and the Holy Spirit. Amen.

6.2   Praying for Wholeness and Healing

In his ministry, Jesus showed God's power at work by making people whole, so prayer for wholeness and healing is at the heart of the Church's prayer. God answers our prayer, but not always in the way we expect. Our wholeness is bound up with our salvation and is a sign of God's new creation. As St Paul says:

If anyone is in Christ, there is a new creation.
The old has passed away: behold, the new has come.

2 Corinthians 5.17

Ransomed, healed, restored, forgiven,
Who like me his praise should sing!
From 'Praise, my soul, the King of heaven' by H. F. Lyte (1793-1847)

Bless the Lord, O my soul
and forget not all his benefits,
Who forgives all our sins
and heals all our infirmities,
Who redeems our life from the Pit
and crowns us with love and compassion.

From Psalm 103

Jesus said, 'Come to me, all who labour and are heavy laden, and
I will give you rest. Take my yoke upon you, and learn from me; for
I am gentle and lowly in heart, and you shall find rest for your souls.
For my yoke is easy, and my burden is light.'

Matthew 11.28—30

Blessèd are you, Sovereign God, gentle and merciful,
creator of heaven and earth:
Your word brought light out of darkness
and daily your Spirit renews the face of the earth.
Your Son, Jesus Christ, brought life and health,
bringing wholeness and joy to a broken world.
Pour out your Spirit on us today
and hear our prayer for those for whom we pray:
heal the sick, raise the fallen,
strengthen the fainthearted,
bring light to those in darkness
and enfold in your mercy those who have no hope.
Reconcile all things in Christ and make them new,
that we may be restored in your image,
renewed in your love
and serve you as sons and daughters in your kingdom.
We make our prayer through your anointed Son,
to whom with you and your lifegiving Spirit
be glory and praise, now and for ever. Amen.

Then pray for any whom you know to be sick in mind or body, those in need of wholeness and healing and those who care for them.

Almighty God,
whose Son revealed in signs and miracles
the wonder of your saving presence:
renew [*N, N… and*] all your people
with your heavenly grace,
and in all our weakness
sustain us by your mighty power,
through Jesus Christ our Lord. Amen.

Then pray for yourself, that God may make you whole, strong and free.

In the name of God and trusting in his might alone,
May I receive Christ's healing touch to make me whole. Amen.

May Christ bring me wholeness of body, mind and spirit,
deliver me from every evil, and give me his peace. Amen.

May the Father of our Lord Jesus Christ grant me
the riches of his grace, his wholeness and his peace. Amen.

May the almighty Lord,
who is a strong tower for all who put their trust in him,
whom all things in heaven, on earth, and under the earth obey,
be now and evermore my defence.
May I believe and trust that the only name under heaven
given for health and salvation
is the name of our Lord Jesus Christ.

6.3　Penitence and Reconciliation

The Church has always recognized that while our baptism into Christ's dying and rising has set us on the way to becoming that new person we are called to be, our continuing self-centredness is always taking us back to the bottom, 'guilty of dust and sinne'. But we are not left there. Whatever we have done, God is ready to offer us a new start, if we acknowledge that we have gone wrong. Like the Father who sees his prodigal son coming back home to ask if he may start again as a hired servant, God is always running out to meet us and embrace us in his loving arms.

> When the younger son came to himself he said, 'I will arise and go to
> my father and I will say to him, "Father, I have sinned against heaven
> and before you; I am no longer worthy to be called your son; treat me
> as one of your hired servants."' And he arose and came to his father.
> But while he was still far off, his father saw him and had compassion
> and ran and embraced him and kissed him. Then the son said to him,
> 'Father, I have sinned against heaven and before you; I am no longer
> worthy to be called your son.' But the father said to his servants,
> 'Quickly, bring out a robe — the best one — and put it on him; put
> a ring on his finger and sandals on his feet. And get the fatted calf
> and kill it, and let us eat and celebrate; for this son of mine was dead
> and is alive again; he was lost and is found!'
>
> *Luke 15.18–24a*

Celebrating the Sacrament of Reconciliation – Making your Confession, as it is still commonly called – puts an end to the separation between us and God, between us and each other, between us and the natural order, and between us and our inner selves. The ministry of reconciliation is one of God's gifts to his world and that power to forgive sins is Jesus' command to his Church. As he breathed on his disciples, Jesus said to them plainly:

> Receive the Holy Spirit. If you forgive the sins of any,
> they are forgiven. If you retain the sins of any, they are retained.
>
> *John 20.22b–23*

It is part of a Christian's discipline in growing in holiness to take sin seriously. How you exercise your responsibility to prepare for the restoration to your baptismal status as a child of God – recognizing that he loves you and is willing you to return to him – is a matter for you to work through.

Sin and its Remedy

The root of sin is self-centredness, putting ourselves and what we want at the heart of our being. Human beings are naturally self-protective, yet are capable of remarkable acts of self-sacrifice. The effect of sin is to separate us from God, from one another, from the natural order and even from our true selves. But it is the glory of human beings to be able to transcend our natural selfishness and put the interests of others before our own. The supreme example of this sacrificial life is Jesus, and in the Lord's Prayer he teaches us to pray to the Father 'Your kingdom come, your will be done', pre-echoing his prayer in the garden of Gethsemane, 'not my will, but yours be done'.

It is by our baptism that we are drawn into Christ's perfect self-offering to the Father. We are baptized into his death, so that dying to sin we may rise to the life of righteousness. But this adoption needs constant re-invigoration. Sin is always drawing us back into self-centred concerns, and we constantly need forgiveness for our failure to live a God-centred life.

So the Church has always taken seriously Christ's command to his disciples to absolve the penitent and free them from the chains of sin by helping people who long to live more godly lives to know the embrace of God's love, set the past behind them and make a fresh start.

At the centre of the Church's penitential celebration is Jesus' parable of the Prodigal Son's return, where it is clear that the Father's compassion rather than the son's change of heart is the gospel – the good news. So although we talk of 'making our confession', with the emphasis on us, the Gospel is always pointing us beyond ourselves to what God has done for us.

The liturgical celebration of the Sacrament of Reconciliation has the proclamation of the Father's love at its heart. It is in the light of this that we are bold enough to acknowledge what we have done – or failed to do – and 'being truly penitent', as the Book of Common Prayer puts it, 'receive the absolution and remission' of all our sins.

The Church of England's tradition in the matter of making a personal confession is 'All may; none must; some should.' There is a basic discipline in thinking carefully about what you have actually done and said and thought in relation to the faith you profess. If you are helped by having to face up to being that person, then regular meetings with a spiritual guide or director and the discipline of having to prepare for making your confession may be important not just in helping you to be honest with yourself but in helping you grow as a person who is becoming more ready to be formed into what God wants you to be.

Choosing a director or confessor is the first step. Your parish priest or chaplain will be ready to advise you, and it may well be that they suggest someone other than themselves. It may be easier for a person you see only four or five times a year to notice growth and change in your spiritual life than for someone who sees you every day or every week. Like a doctor, your director is there to help diagnose what is going awry, and is enormously dependent on the information you give. They can only help if you give them the complete picture.

Your spiritual director will help you to prepare. Be honest about what you have done or failed to do. Don't try and hide behind generalizations – 'I'm the sort of person who tends to …' Say simply 'I told that lie to get out of a difficulty, and I did it again last Tuesday.' And don't try and make excuses: we are who we are, and God longs for an honest relationship with us that he can help us grow up a bit.

Preparing

When you come to prepare to make your confession, you may like to use one or more of the following.

> Bless the Lord, O my soul,
> and all that is within me bless his holy name.
> Bless the Lord, O my soul,
> and forget not all his benefits;
> Who forgives all your sins
> and heals all your infirmities;
> Who redeems your life from the Pit
> and crowns you with faithful love and compassion.
>
> *Psalm 103.1–4*

> Whatever gain I had, these I have come to regard as loss because of Christ. Indeed I count everything as loss because of the surpassing value of knowing Christ Jesus my Lord. For his sake I have suffered the loss of all things and I regard them as refuse, in order that I may gain Christ and be found in him, not having a righteousness of my own that comes from the law, but one that comes through faith in Christ, the righteousness from God based on faith; that I may know him and the power of his resurrection, and may share his sufferings, becoming like him in his death, that if possible I may attain the resurrection from the dead.
>
> *Philippians 3.7–11*

6.4 A Form of Confession

When you are ready, go and kneel down by the priest and say:

Bless me, for I have sinned.

When the priest has given you a blessing, say:

I confess to God almighty, before the whole company of heaven
and before you,
that I have sinned in thought, word, deed and by omission,
through my fault, my own fault, my most grievous fault.
Especially since my last confession, which was ... ago,
I confess that ...

*Say how long it was since your last confession: if this is your first confession, say 'since
my baptism'. Then confess your sins, and after you have finished say:*

For these and all my other sins that I cannot now remember,
I am very sorry, firmly resolve not to sin again,
humbly ask pardon of God,
and of you advice, penance and absolution.

*The priest will bless you. Listen to any advice the priest gives you, and what prayer
or other penance you are asked to use to show that you are really sorry. Then the priest
will say:*

Words of Absolution

Our Lord Jesus Christ, who hath left power to his Church to absolve
all sinners who truly repent and believe in him, of his great mercy
forgive thee thine offences: And by his authority committed unto me,
I absolve thee from all thy sins, in the name of the Father, and of the
Son, and of the Holy Ghost. Amen.

God has put away your sin; go in peace and pray for me, a sinner too.

6.5 Learning for Life

Prayer and study go hand in hand: there is a reflective way of reading the Bible that Christians have always practised, especially reading the psalms which were the prayers of Jesus himself.

> This is the royal law;
> These are the lively oracles of God.
>> *Words spoken in the Coronation rite, as the Sovereign is handed the Bible*

> Your word is a lantern to my feet and a light upon our path.
>> *Psalm 119.105*

> Almighty God,
> we thank you for the gift of your holy word.
> May it be a lantern to our feet, a light to our paths,
> and a strength to our lives.
> Take us and use us to love and serve all your people
> in the power of the Holy Spirit
> and in the name of your Son, Jesus Christ our Lord.

But Learning for Life is not just about reading the Bible. It is also about learning God's ways so that they become not just something we are always looking up in a book, but rather how we instinctively do things. In the Jewish tradition, there is much about feeding on the Law:

> How sweet are your words on my tongue!
> They are sweeter than honey to my mouth.
>> *Psalm 119.103*

But more important was to live it.

> Moses said, 'Lay up these words of mine in your heart and soul, and you shall bind them as a sign on your hand and fix them as frontlets between your eyes. Teach them to your children, talking about them when you are sitting in your house and when you are walking by the way, and when you lie down and when you rise.'
>> *Deuteronomy 11.18–21*

But study alone is not enough. To think of entering the mind of God was to approach an inscrutable mystery.

> Job said, 'Where shall wisdom be found, and where is the place of understanding? Mortals do not know the way to it and it is not found in the land of the living. God understands the way of it and he knows its place. For he looks to the ends of the earth and sees everything under the heavens. And he said, "Truly, the fear of the Lord, that is wisdom; and to depart from evil is understanding."'

Job 28.12–13, 24,28

For us, the Word of God is not the Law, or even the whole Bible. The living Word is Jesus himself. So feeding on him, learning to think and speak his thoughts and words, not our own, is what is important. 'Have this mind among yourselves,' says St Paul, 'that was in Christ Jesus.'

	The Word of life which was from the beginning
All	*We proclaim to you.*
	The darkness is passing away
	and the true light is already shining.
All	*The Word of life which was from the beginning.*
	That which we heard, which we saw with our eyes,
	and touched with our own hands,
All	*We proclaim to you.*
	For our fellowship is with the Father,
	and with his Son, Jesus Christ our Lord.
All	*The Word of life, which was from the beginning,*
	we proclaim to you.

O God, by whose command the order of time runs its course:
forgive our impatience, perfect our faith
and, while we await the fulfilment of your promise,
grant us to have a good hope because of your Word,
even Jesus Christ our Lord.

Gregory Nazianzus (c.330–390)

6.6 Family and Relationships

The model of our relationships is the Divine Love, expressed in the communion of the persons of the Holy Trinity. Our affection for one another does not only derive from our relationship with God: it is to reflect it.

Love of the Father, love of God the Son,
From whom all came, in whom was all begun;
Who formest heavenly beauty out of strife,
Creation's whole desire and breath of life.

Thou the all-holy, thou supreme in might,
Thou dost give peace, thy presence maketh right;
Thou with thy favour all things dost enfold,
With thine all-kindness free from harm wilt hold.

Hope of all comfort, splendour of all aid,
That dost not fail nor leave the heart afraid:
To all that cry thou dost all help afford,
The Angels' armour and the Saints' reward.

Purest and highest, wisest and most just;
There is no truth, save only in thy trust;
Thou dost the mind from earthly dreams recall,
And bring through Christ to him from whom are all.

Eternal glory, all men thee adore,
Who art and shalt be worshipped evermore:
Us whom thou madest, comfort with thy might,
And lead us to enjoy the heavenly light.

12th century, tr. for the Yattendon Hymnal

Merciful God,
you have prepared for those who love you
such good things as pass our understanding:
pour into our hearts such love toward you
that we, loving you in all things and above all things,
may obtain your promises,
which exceed all that we can desire;
through Jesus Christ your Son our Lord,
who is alive and reigns with you,
in the unity of the Holy Spirit,
one God, now and for ever.

A Song of Solomon

Set me as a seal upon your heart,
as a seal upon your arm;

For love is strong as death, passion fierce as the grave;
its flashes are flashes of fire, a raging flame.

Many waters cannot quench love,
neither can the floods drown it.

If all the wealth of our house were offered for love,
it would be utterly scorned.

Song of Solomon 8.6—7

Beloved, let us love one another, because love is from God; everyone
who loves is born of God and knows God; for God is love. We love
because God first loved us. Those who say 'I love God', and hate their
brothers or sisters, are liars; for those who do not love a brother or sister
whom they have seen, cannot love God whom they have not seen.

I John 4.7,19—20

All praise and blessing to you, God of love,
creator of the universe,
maker of man and woman in your likeness,
source of blessing for married life.
All praise to you, for you have created
courtship and marriage,
joy and gladness,
feasting and laughter,
pleasure and delight.
May your blessing come in full on *N* and *N*.
Let their love for each other be a seal upon their hearts
and a crown upon their heads.
Bless them in their work and in their companionship;
awake and asleep,
in joy and in sorrow,
in life and in death.
May they reach old age in the company of friends
and feast at last at the table in your eternal kingdom,
through Jesus Christ our Lord.

Adapted from Common Worship: Pastoral Services

But the most intimate relationship into which we are drawn is the relationship between the Father and the Son on which we eavesdrop in chapters 14 to 17 of St John's Gospel.

I do not pray for these only, but for those who believe in me through
their word, that they may all be one; even as thou, Father, art in me
and I in thee, that they also may be in us …

John 17.20–21

It is St Paul's hymn to love that is probably best known.

If I speak in the tongues of men and of angels, but have not love
I am a noisy gong or a tinkling cymbal.
And if I have prophetic powers,
And understand all mysteries and all knowledge,
But have not love, I am nothing.
If I give away all I have, and if I deliver my body to be burned,
But have not love, I gain nothing.

Love is patient and kind,
love is not jealous or boastful; it is not arrogant or rude.
Love does not insist on its own way;
it is not irritable or resentful;
It does not rejoice in wrong, but rejoices in the right.
Love bears all things, believes all things,
hopes all things, endures all things.

Love never ends;
As for prophecies, they will pass away;
As for tongues, they will cease;
As for knowledge, it will pass away.
Now we know only in part
and we prophesy only in part,
But when the perfect comes,
the imperfect will pass away.

When I was a child, I spoke like a child,
I thought like a child, I reasoned like a child;
But when I became a man,
I gave up childish ways.
For now we see in a mirror dimly,
but then face to face.
Now I know in part;
then I shall understand fully, even as I have been fully understood.

So faith, hope, love abide, these three;
but the greatest of these is love.

1 Corinthians 13

Almighty and everlasting God, give unto us the increase of faith,
hope, and charity;
and, that we may obtain that which thou dost promise,
make us to love that which thou dost command;
through Jesus Christ our Lord.

A Celtic prayer for blessing a house

God bless the house from ground to stay,
From beam to wall and all the way,
From head to post, from ridge to clay,
From balk to roof-tree let it stay,
From found to top and every day
God bless both fore and aft, I pray,
Nor from the house God's blessing stray,
From top to toe the blessing go.

6.7 Vocation – What are my Gifts?

However insignificant we feel, Isaiah assures us that God knows us.

> I have called you by name, you are mine.
>
> *Isaiah 43.1*

From his first moments, the prophet Jeremiah knows that he has been called by God to serve him.

> Now the word of the Lord came to me, saying, 'Before I formed you in the womb, I knew you. And before you were born I consecrated you. I appointed you a prophet to the nations.' Then I said, 'Ah, Lord God! Truly I do not know how to speak, for I am only a youth.' But the Lord said to me, 'Do not say "I am only a youth", for you shall go to all to whom I send you, and you shall speak whatever I command you. Do not be afraid of them for I am with you to deliver,' says the Lord.
>
> *Jeremiah 1.4–6*

Jesus' parable of the talents (Matthew 25.14–29) gives us a clear picture that the gifts we have been given are to be used for God, and not just hoarded.

> For it will be as when a man going on a journey called his servants and entrusted to them his property; to one he gave five talents, to another two, to another one, to each according to his ability.

When the master returns, he calls his servants to see how they have used what they were given, and commends those who have traded and doubled their money.

> Well done, good and faithful servant; you have been faithful over little, I will set you over much; enter into the joy of your master.

But when the one who was afraid of losing what he had been given and so hid the talent in a
hole in the ground gave it back without even any bank interest, the master took it from him,
and said:

> To everyone who has will more be given, and he will have abundance;
> but from him who has not, even what he has will be taken away.

> Keep us, O Lord,
> while we tarry on this earth,
> in a serious seeking after you,
> and in an affectionate walking with you,
> every day of our lives;
> that when you come,
> we may be found not hiding our talent,
> nor serving the flesh,
> nor yet asleep with our lamp unfurnished,
> but waiting and longing for our Lord,
> our glorious God for ever.

Richard Baxter (1615-1691)

The promise of God is not that each individual has a full supply of all the gifts that there
are, but that the members of his Church together have all they need. So by learning to share
them, we can build up the body of Christ.

> There are varieties of gifts but the same Spirit; and there are varieties
> of service but the same Lord; and there are varieties of activities but it
> is the same God who inspires them all in everyone. To each is given
> the manifestation of the Spirit for the common good.

> For just as the body is one and has many members, and all the
> members of the body, though many, are one body, so it is with Christ.
> For in the one Spirit we were all baptized into one body – Jews or
> Greeks, slaves or free – and we were all made to drink of one spirit.

> Now you are the body of Christ and individually members of it.
> And God has appointed in the church first apostles, second prophets,
> third teachers, then workers of miracles, then healers, helpers,
> administrators, speakers in various kinds of tongues. Are all apostles?
> Are all prophets? Are all teachers?

1 Corinthians 12.4–7,12–13, 27–29

Discerning the gifts each of us have is not something that is easy to do on our own. That is why it is within the company of the faithful that others may point out to us gifts we did not know we had, and why discernment of the gifts for ordained ministry is always the responsibility of the whole Church. What is required is that we offer ourselves, and let God do with us what he wills.

When Isaiah saw a vision of the majesty of God in the Temple, he was struck dumb by his unworthiness. But then he heard the voice of the Lord, saying:

Whom shall I send and who will go for us?

Then he said:

Here am I! Send me.

Lord,
Take my hands and work with them;
Take my lips and speak through them;
Take my mind and think with it;
Take my heart and set it on fire
    with love for you and all creation.

Charles Wesley's hymn prays the same prayer for a renewed discipleship.

O Thou who camest from above
The fire celestial to impart,
Kindle a flame of sacred love
On the mean altar of my heart!

There let it for thy glory burn
With inextinguishable blaze,
And trembling to its source return
In humble prayer and fervent praise.

Jesus, confirm my heart's desire
To work, and speak, and think for thee;
Still let me guard the holy fire,
And still stir up the gift in me.

Ready for all thy perfect will,
My acts of faith and love repeat,
Till death thy endless mercies seal,
And make my sacrifice complete.   *Charles Wesley (1707–1788)*

Here, Lord, is my life:
I place it on the altar today.
Use it as you will.

Albert Schweitzer (1875-1965)

But it is not just that we are to use the gifts God has given us, he also needs us to bring his will into being. We cannot pray and do nothing. When we pray: 'Your kingdom come; your will be done, on earth as in heaven', we are offering ourselves as agents of God's transforming love.

Christ has no body now on earth but ours,
no hands but ours, no feet but ours.
Ours are the eyes though which Christ's compassion is to look out
    on the world;
ours are the feet with which he is to go about doing good;
ours are the hands by which he is to bless his people,
now and to the end of the ages.

St Teresa of Avila (1515-1582)

Remember, O Lord, what thou hast wrought in us
    and not what we deserve;
and as thou hast called us to thy service,
    make us worthy of our calling;
through Jesus Christ our Lord.

The Prayer Book as proposed in 1928

6.8   Praying for Unity in Christ

Jesus prayed that his followers might be one. The scandal of disunity weakens both the witness and the mission of the Church. Christians, who claim to make their prayer 'through Jesus Christ our Lord', should pray seriously for this unity. Prayers are often offered on Thursdays, remembering the Prayer of Jesus at the Last Supper. Sometimes prayers take place around a unity candle.

Jesus said, 'Holy Father, keep them in thy name, which thou hast given me, that they may be one, even as you and I are one.'

John 17.11

Lord Jesus Christ,
who said to your apostles,
Peace I leave with you, my peace I give to you:
look not on our sins but on the faith of your Church
and grant it the peace and unity of your kingdom;
where you are alive and reign with the Father
in the unity of the Holy Spirit,
one God, now and for ever.

Jesus prayed that his followers may all be one. In the power of the Spirit, we join our prayers with his:

O God, the Father of our Lord Jesus Christ,
our only Saviour, the Prince of Peace:
give us grace seriously to lay to heart
the great dangers we are in by our unhappy divisions.
Take away all hatred and prejudice,
and whatever else may hinder us
from godly union and concord;
that, as there is but one body and one Spirit
and one hope of our calling,
one Lord, one faith, one baptism,
one God and Father of us all,
so we may henceforth be all of one heart and of one soul,
united in one holy bond of truth and peace, of faith and charity,
and may with one mind and one mouth glorify you;
through Jesus Christ our Lord.

Jesus said:
   I am the vine and you are the branches.
We pray his words:
All   *Abide in me as I abide in you.*
   As the Father has loved me, so have I loved you.
All   *Abide in me as I abide in you.*
   No one has greater love than this,
   to lay down one's life for one's friends.
All   *Abide in me as I abide in you.*
   You are my friends if you do what I command you;
   love one another as I have loved you.
All   *Abide in me as I abide in you.*

All   *Our Father ...*

   Behold how good and pleasant it is
   to dwell together in unity.

                                                      Psalm 133.1

6.9　Hospitality

Part of our responsibility for living the faith is to share our home and our table. Those who are married need to think who are the single people who may be on their own for an anniversary or occasion. Those who are single are often naturally hospitable: cooking for one, and sitting down to a meal on your own, hardly seems right. And eating together binds people to one another: it is difficult for sullen hostility to remain when you share a meal.

> Better a dinner of herbs where love is,
> Than a fatted ox and hatred with it.
>
> *Proverbs 15.17*

The early Church was distinctive for its fellowship, and hospitality is one of the duties required of bishops (1 Timothy 3.2).

> And all who believed were together and had all things in common;
> and they sold their possessions and goods, and distributed them to all,
> as any had need. And day by day, attending the temple together and
> breaking bread in their homes, they partook of food with glad and
> generous hearts, praising God and having favour with all the people.
>
> *Acts 2.44–47*

> Do not neglect to show hospitality to strangers, for thereby some
> have entertained angels unawares.
>
> *Hebrews 13.2*

> Let every guest be received as Christ himself.
>
> *Rule of St Benedict*

If you lay an extra place at table say:
> And one for Elijah.

> Mensae coelestis participes faciat nos Rex aeternae gloriae.
> *May the King of eternal glory make us partakers of the heavenly table too.*
> *The final blessing of the traditional Benedictine Grace before meals*

> Come Lord Jesus, be our guest,
> And may our meal by thee be blest.
>
> *Attributed to Martin Luther (1483–1546)*

> Be present at our table, Lord;
> Be here and everywhere adored.
> Thy creatures bless, and grant that we
> In paradise may feast with thee.　*John Wesley (1703–1791)*

6.10 Going on a Journey

Some journeys are routine, but even they may have dangers. Others are journeys that will bring new experiences. These prayers will help you be aware of God's presence and protection, and will help you keep alert to new horizons.

You may use parts of one or other of these psalms.

Psalm 121

> I lift up my eyes to the hills;
> from where is my help to come?
>
> My help comes from the Lord,
> the maker of heaven and earth.
>
> He will not suffer your foot to stumble;
> he who watches over you will not sleep.
>
> Behold, he who keeps watch over Israel
> shall neither slumber nor sleep.
>
> The Lord himself watches over you;
> the Lord is your shade at your right hand,
>
> So that the sun shall not strike you by day,
> neither the moon by night.
>
> The Lord shall keep you from all evil;
> it is he who shall keep your soul.
>
> The Lord shall keep watch over your going out
>   and your coming in,
> from this time forth for evermore.

From Psalm 139

O Lord, you have searched me out and known me;
you know my sitting down and my rising up;
    you discern my thoughts from afar.

You mark out my journeys and my resting place
and are acquainted with all my ways.

For there is not a word on my tongue,
but you, O Lord, know it altogether.

You encompass me behind and before
and lay your hand upon me.

Such knowledge is too wonderful for me,
so high that I cannot attain it.

Where can I go then from your spirit?
Or where can I flee from your presence?

If I climb up to heaven, you are there;
if I make the grave my bed, you are there also.

If I take the wings of the morning
and dwell in the uttermost parts of the sea,

Even there your hand shall lead me,
your right hand hold me fast.

If I say, 'Surely the darkness will cover me
and the light around me turn to night,'

Even darkness is no darkness with you;
    the night is as clear as the day;
darkness and light to you are both alike.

You may use these verses, familiar from the marriage service and from well known psalms, to introduce prayer for those who are journeying.

O Lord, save your servants,
Who put their trust in you.

Send them help from your holy sanctuary,
And ever more mightily defend them.

Be unto them, O Lord, a strong tower
From the face of the enemy.

Show them your ways, O Lord,
And teach them your paths.

O God, give your angels charge over them,
To keep them in all their ways.

This fifteenth-century poem may be used:

Tarry no longer; t'ward thine heritage
haste on thy way, and be of right good cheer.
Go each day onward on thy pilgrimage;
think how short time thou shalt abide here.
Thy place is bigged above the starres clear,
none earthly palace wrought in so stately wise.
Come on, my friend, my brother most entere!
For thee I offered my blood in sacrifice.

John Lydgate (c.1370-1447)

6.11 When Death Comes

When we hear the news of someone's death we often feel helpless. Our first responsibility is to pray — to pray for the one who has died, to pray for those who will be overwhelmed by grief, and to pray for ourselves, that when death comes to us, we may be ready to come before God.

These prayers may be used on hearing the news of a death, or on the day of the funeral if you are not able to be present, or to help prepare for your own death.

If it seems appropriate, they might be adapted to use with someone who is very close to death.

> I know that my redeemer liveth
> and he shall stand at the last day.
>
> For Lo, I tell you a mystery.
> We shall not all sleep, but we shall be changed.
> For the trumpet shall sound and the dead will be raised;
> and we shall be changed.

Psalm 23 may be used.

> The Lord is my shepherd;
> therefore can I lack nothing.
>
> He makes me lie down in green pastures
> and leads me beside still waters.
>
> He shall refresh my soul
> and guide me in the paths of righteousness for his name's sake.
>
> Though I walk through the valley of the shadow of death,
>   I will fear no evil;
> for you are with me;
>   your rod and your staff, they comfort me.
>
> You spread a table before me
>   in the presence of those who trouble me;
> you have anointed my head with oil
>   and my cup shall be full.
>
> Surely goodness and loving mercy shall follow me
>   all the days of my life,
> and I will dwell in the house of the Lord for ever.

One of these readings may be suitable.

For I am sure that neither death, nor life, nor angels, nor principalities, nor things present, nor things to come, nor powers, nor height, nor depth, nor anything else in all creation, will be able to separate us from the love of God which is in Christ Jesus our Lord.

Romans 8.39

Jesus said to Martha, 'I am the resurrection and the life. Those who believe in me, even though they die, yet shall they live, and everyone who lives and believes in me will never die. Do you believe this?' She said to him, 'Yes, Lord, I believe that you are the Messiah, the Son of God, the one coming into the world.'

John 11.25—26

Jesus said, 'Do not let your hearts be troubled. Believe in God, believe also in me. In my Father's house are many dwelling places. If it were not so, would I have told you that I go to prepare a place for you? And if I go and prepare a place for you, I will come again and will take you to myself, so that where I am, there you may be also. I am the way, and the truth, and the life. No one comes to the Father except through me. If you know me, you will know my Father also. From now on, you do know him and have seen him.'

John 14.1—3,6—7

He wants not friends that hath thy love,
and may converse and walk with thee
and with thy saints, here and above,
with whom for ever I must be.

Within the fellowship of saints
is wisdom, safety, and delight;
and when my heart declines and faints,
it's raised by their heat and light.

As for my friends, they are not lost:
the several vessels of thy fleet
though parted now, by tempests tossed,
shall safely in the haven meet.

Still we are centred all in thee,
members, though distant, of one Head;
in the same family we be,
by the same faith and spirit led.

Before thy throne we daily meet
as joint-petitioners to thee;
in spirit we each other greet,
and shall again each other see.

The heavenly hosts, world without end,
shall be my company above;
and thou, my best and surest Friend,
who shall divide me from thy love?

Richard Baxter (1615-1691)

Intercession may be offered.

Lord, have mercy.
Christ, have mercy.
Lord, have mercy.

Heavenly Father,
into whose hands Jesus Christ commended his spirit at the last hour:
into those same hands we now commend your servant *N.*,
that death may be for *him/her*
the gate to life and to eternal fellowship with you;
through Jesus Christ our Lord. Amen.

Lord Jesus, remember us in your kingdom and teach us to pray:

Our Father ...

You may use one or more of these prayers of commendation.

Into your hands, O merciful Saviour,
we commend your servant N.
Acknowledge, we pray, a sheep of your own fold,
a lamb of your own flock,
a sinner of your own redeeming.
Enfold *him/her* in the arms of thy mercy,
in the blessed rest of everlasting peace
and in the glorious company of the saints in light. Amen.

Go forth upon your journey from this world, O Christian soul:
in the name of God the Father who created you. Amen.
In the name of Jesus Christ who suffered for you. Amen.
In the name of the Holy Spirit who strengthens you. Amen.
In communion with the blessèd saints,
with the angels and archangels and all the heavenly host.
May your portion this day be in peace
and your dwelling in the heavenly Jerusalem. Amen.

N., our companion in faith and *brother/sister* in Christ,
  we entrust you to God who created you.
May you return to the Most High who formed you
  from the dust of the earth.
May the angels and the saints come to meet you
  as you go forth from this life.
May Christ, who was crucified for you,
  take you into his Kingdom.
May Christ the Good Shepherd
  give you a place within his flock.
May Christ forgive you your sins
  and keep you among his people.
May you see your Redeemer face to face
  and delight in the vision of God for ever. Amen.

Give rest, O Christ, to your servants with your saints,
where sorrow and pain are no more, neither sighing,
but life everlasting.

You only are immortal, the creator and maker of all:
and we are mortal, formed from the dust of the earth,
and unto the earth shall we return;
for so you did ordain when you created me, saying,
'Dust thou art, and unto dust shalt thou return.'
All we go down into the dust;
and weeping o'er the grave, we make our song:
'Alleluia, Alleluia, Alleluia.'

Give rest, O Christ, to your servants with your saints,
where sorrow and pain are no more, neither sighing,
but life everlasting.

Russian kontakion for the dead

N., may Christ give you rest in the land of the living
and open for you the gates of paradise;
may he receive you as a citizen of the Kingdom,
and grant you forgiveness of your sins:
for you were his friend.

In conclusion:

Rest eternal grant unto *him/her*, O Lord,
and let light perpetual shine upon *him/her*.

May *he/she*, with all the faithful departed, rest in peace
and rise in glory. Amen.

7 Prayer Through the Ages

7.1 Prayer

Prayer the Churches banquet, Angels age,
  Gods breath in man returning to his birth,
  The soul in paraphrase, heart in pilgrimage,
The Christian plummet sounding heav'n and earth;

Engine against th' Almightie, sinners towre,
  Reversed thunder, Christ-side-piercing spear,
  The six-daies world-transposing in an hour,
A kinde of tune, which all things heare and fear;

Softnesse, and peace, and joy, and love, and blisse,
  Exalted Manna, gladnesse of the best,
  Heaven in ordinarie, man well drest,
The milkie way, the bird of Paradise,

  Church-bels beyond the starres heard, the souls bloud,
  The land of spices; something understood.

George Herbert (1593-1633)

Come, Holy Spirit, fill the hearts of your faithful people
and kindle in us the fire of your love.

Traditional invocation of the Holy Spirit at the start of prayer

Moments of great calm
Kneeling before an altar
Of wood in a stone church
In summer, waiting for the God
To speak; the air a staircase
For silence ...

R. S. Thomas (1913-2001), an extract from 'Kneeling'

7.2   Praise and Thanksgiving

Antiphon

> Let all the world in every corner sing,
> > *My God and King.*

> The heavens are not too high,
> His praise may thither fly;
> The earth is not too low,
> His praises there may grow.

> Let all the world in every corner sing,
> > *My God and King.*

> The Church with psalms must shout,
> No door can keep them out;
> But above all, the heart
> Must bear the longest part.

> Let all the world in every corner sing,
> > *My God and King.*

George Herbert (1593-1633)

In the morning:

> Glory to thee, who safe hast kept
> And hast refreshed me while I slept;
> Grant, Lord, when I from death shall wake
> I may of endless heaven partake.

In the evening:

> Glory to thee, my God this night
> For all the blessings of the light;
> Keep me, O keep me, King of Kings,
> Beneath thine own almighty wings.

The Doxology, often sung as a round to Tallis' Canon as a Grace:

Praise God from whom all blessings flow,
Praise him all creatures here below;
Praise him above ye heavenly host;
Praise Father, Son and Holy Ghost.

Thomas Ken (1637-1711)

The General Thanksgiving

Almighty God, Father of all mercies, we thine unworthy servants do give thee most humble and hearty thanks for all thy goodness and loving-kindness to us, and to all men. We bless thee for our creation, preservation, and all the blessings of this life; but above all, for thine inestimable love in the redemption of the world by our Lord Jesus Christ; for the means of grace, and for the hope of glory. And, we beseech thee, give us that due sense of all thy mercies that our hearts may be unfeignèdly thankful, and that we show forth thy praise, not only with our lips, but in our lives; by giving up ourselves to thy service, and by walking before thee in holiness and righteousness all our days; through Jesus Christ our Lord, to whom with thee and the Holy Ghost be all honour and glory, world without end. Amen.

Edward Reynolds, Bishop of Norwich (1599-1676)

To God the Father, who loved us and made us accepted in the Beloved:
To God the Son, who loved us and loosed us from our sins
    in his own blood:
To God the Holy Spirit, who sheds the love of God abroad
    in our hearts:
To the one true God be all love and all glory, for time and for eternity.
    Amen.

Thomas Ken (1637-1711)

7.3 The Majesty and Presence of God

Job answered the Lord: 'I know that you can do all things and that no
purpose of yours can be thwarted. "Who is this that hides counsel
without knowledge?" Therefore, I have uttered what I did not
understand; things too wonderful for me which I did not know.
"Hear, and I will speak; I will question you, and you declare to me."
I had heard of you by the hearing of the ear, but now my eye sees you;
therefore I despise myself, and repent in dust and ashes.'

Job 42.1–6

How shall I sing that majesty
which angels do admire?
Let dust in dust and silence lie;
sing, sing, ye heavenly choir.
Thousands of thousands stand around
thy throne, O God most high;
ten thousand times ten thousand sound
thy praise; but who am I?

Thy brightness unto them appears,
whilst I thy footsteps trace;
a sound of God comes to my ears,
but they behold thy face:
They sing, because thou art their sun.
Lord, send a beam on me;
For where heaven is but once begun,
There alleluias be.

Enlighten with faith's light my heart,
inflame it with love's fire,
then shall I sing and take my part
with that celestial choir.
I shall, I fear, be dark and cold,
with all my fire and light;
yet when thou dost accept their gold,
Lord, treasure up my mite.

How great a being, Lord, is thine,
which doth all beings keep!
Thy knowledge is the only line
to sound so vast a deep.
Thou art a sea without a shore,
A sun without a sphere;
thy time is now and evermore,
thy place is everywhere.

John Mason (c.1645-1694)

The glory of God is a living person
and the life of man is the vision of God.

Irenaeus of Lyons (c.130-c.202)

I said to the man who stood at the Gate of the Year, 'Give me a light
that I may tread safely into the unknown.' And he replied, 'Go out
into the darkness, and put your hand into the Hand of God. That
shall be to you better than light, and safer than a known way.'

*Louise Haskins (1875-1958), quoted by King George VI
in his Christmas Broadcast, 1939*

Christ is the morning star
Who when the darkness of this world is passed
Brings to his saints the promise of light of life
And opens everlasting day.

The Venerable Bede (673-735)

Thus says the Lord who created you, O Jacob,
He who formed you, O Israel:
'Fear not, for I have redeemed you;
I have called you by name, you are mine.'

Isaiah 43.1

I believe in the sun, even if it does not shine.
I believe in love, even if I do not feel it.
I believe in God, even if I do not see him.

*Written on the wall of the Warsaw ghetto
by an unknown young Jew, c. 1942*

7.4   Penitence and Forgiveness

The returning son says to his father:

> Father, I have sinned against heaven and in thy sight, and am no more
> worthy to be called thy son.
>
> *Luke 15.21*

The penitent thief on the cross says to Jesus:

> Jesus, remember me when you come into your kingdom.
>
> *Luke 23.42*

> As they were stoning Stephen, he prayed, 'Lord Jesus, receive my
> spirit.' And he knelt down and cried with a loud voice:
> 'Lord, do not hold this sin against them.'
>
> *Acts 7.59*

> O Lord, who hast mercy upon all, take away from me my sins, and
> mercifully kindle in me the fire of thy Holy Spirit; take away from me
> the heart of stone, and give me a heart of flesh, a heart to love and
> adore thee, a heart to delight in thee, to follow and to enjoy thee, for
> Christ's sake.
>
> *St Ambrose of Milan (339-397)*

> Forgive me my sins, O Lord;
> forgive me the sins of my youth and of my age,
> the sins of my soul and the sins of my body,
> my secret and my whispering sins,
> my presumptuous and my crying sins,
> the sins I have done to please myself
> and the sins I have done to please others.
> Forgive me the sins which I know,
> and those sins which I know not;
> forgive them, O Lord,
> forgive them of thy great goodness.
>
> *Lancelot Andrewes (1555-1626)*

Lord, for thy tender mercies' sake, lay not our sins to our charge; but forgive that is past and give us grace to amend our sinful lives; to decline from sin and incline to virtue, that we may walk with a perfect heart before thee now and evermore.

Nicholas Ridley (c.1500-1555)

O Lord, remember not only the men and women of good will, but also those of ill will. But do not remember all the suffering they have inflicted on us; remember instead the fruits we have bought, thanks to this suffering – our comradeship, our loyalty, our humility, our courage, our generosity, the greatness of heart which has grown out of all this; and when they come to judgement, let all the fruits which we have borne be for their forgiveness.

An unknown prisoner in Ravensbrück concentration camp

For our enemies:

O Lord our God, and God of our Fathers, we pray that, in the moment of our victory, we may remember the legend handed down to us by our Doctors: that when, after the crossing of the Red Sea, Miriam raised her voice in exultation and the angels at the Throne of thy Glory began to take up the refrain, Thou didst rebuke them, saying: 'What! My children are drowning, and would you sing?'

Written by a rabbi for Armistice Day,
after the midrash by Rabbi Johanan, AD 279

O Lord our God,
grant us grace to desire thee with our whole heart;
that so desiring, we may seek, and, seeking find thee;
and so finding thee may love thee;
and loving thee, may hate those sins that separate us from thee,
for the sake of Jesus Christ our Lord.

St Anselm (1033-1109)

7.5 Anger and Resentment

O God, why have you utterly disowned us?
Why does your anger burn against the sheep of your pasture?

Remember your congregation that you purchased of old,
the tribe you redeemed for your own possession,
    and Mount Zion where you dwelt.

Hasten your steps towards the endless ruins,
where the enemy has laid waste all your sanctuary.

Your adversaries roared in the place of your worship;
they set up their banners as tokens of victory.

Like men brandishing axes on high in a thicket of trees,
all her carved work they smashed down with hatchet and hammer.

They set fire to your holy place;
they defiled the dwelling place of your name
    and razed it to the ground.

They said in their heart, 'Let us make havoc of them altogether,'
and they burned down all the sanctuaries of God in the land.

There are no signs to see, not one prophet left,
not one among us who knows how long.

How long, O God, will the adversary scoff?
Shall the enemy blaspheme your name for ever?

Why have you withheld your hand
and hidden your right hand in your bosom?

Remember now, Lord, how the enemy scoffed,
how a foolish people despised your name.

Do not give to wild beasts the soul of your turtle dove;
forget not the lives of your poor for ever.

Look upon your creation, for the earth is full of darkness,
full of the haunts of violence.

Let not the oppressed turn away ashamed,
but let the poor and needy praise your name.

Arise, O God, maintain your own cause;
remember how fools revile you all the day long.

Forget not the clamour of your adversaries,
the tumult of your enemies that ascends continually.

Psalm 74.1–10, 17–22

Righteous God, holy Redeemer,
renew your broken people with your Holy Spirit,
give them a vision of the coming dawn
and the courage to walk your narrow way,
that they may be a sign of hope to the needy
and proclaim the gracious name of Jesus Christ our Lord.

Michael Vasey (1946–1998)

You, O Lord, reign for ever
Your throne endures from generation to generation
But why do you always forget us?
Why do you forsake us so long?

You have turned a blind eye to your creation
You have abandoned your own children
The skulls in the jungle lie looking up to you in heaven
Do you see them, O Lord?
The scattered, wrecked bones speak for themselves
The widows and orphans

Lord, have you condemned us to death?
Have you no more love for us?
Have you closed your eyes to us?
We cry for your help
Why do you not listen to our cry?

But you are our God, our Lord
Bring us back to you, O God
Bring us back to you if you can, O Lord. Amen

The lament of a Sudanese Christian
after forty years of civil war

God our deliverer,
defender of the poor and needy;
when the foundations of the earth are shaking,
give strength to your people to uphold justice and fight all wrong,
in the name of your son, Jesus Christ our Lord.

David Stancliffe (1942-)

7.6 Delight in the Creation

On tasting any fruit for the first time in the season; or entering a new house, or wearing new clothes; and on birthdays or other special anniversaries:

> Blessed art thou, O Lord our God, King of the Universe,
> who has kept us in life, and has preserved us,
> and has enabled us to reach this season.

On seeing deformed persons:

> Blessed art thou, O Lord our God, King of the Universe,
> who variest the form of thy creatures.

From the Marriage Service; and for remembrance in old age by the married:

> Blessed art thou, O Lord our God, King of the Universe,
> who hast created joy and gladness, bridegroom and bride,
> mirth and exultation, pleasure and delight,
> love, brotherhood, peace and fellowship.
> Blessed art thou, O Lord, who makest the bridegroom to rejoice
>   with the bride.   *The Hebrew Prayer Book*

A Gaelic blessing on a house:

> The peace of God, the peace of men,
> The peace of Columba kindly,
> The peace of Mary mild, the loving,
> The peace of Christ, King of tenderness,
>   The peace of Christ, King of tenderness;
>
> Be upon each window, upon each door,
> Upon each hole that lets in light,
> Upon the four corners of my house,
> Upon the four corners of my bed,
>   Upon the four corners of my bed;
>
> Upon each thing my eye takes in,
> Upon each thing my mouth takes in,
> Upon my body that is of earth,
> And upon my soul that comes from on high,
>   Upon my body that is of earth,
>   And upon my soul that comes from on high.

O God, make the door of this house wide enough
to receive all who need human love and fellowship;
and narrow enough to shut out all envy, pride and hate.
Make its threshold smooth enough to be no stumbling
    block to children, nor to straying feet,
but rugged enough to turn back the tempter's power:
make it a gateway to thy eternal kingdom.

Thomas Ken (1637–1711), over the door of a hospital

Singing is the heartbeat of the human response to the Creator:

Reasons briefly set down by th'auctor, to perswade every one to learn to sing.

First it is a knowledge easily taught, and quickly learned where there
is a good master and an apt Scoller.

2 The exercise of singing is delightfull to Nature and good to
preserve the health of Man.

3 It doth strengthen all the parts of the brest, and doth open the pipes.

4 It is a singular good remedie for a stutting & stammering in the
speech.

5 It is the best means to procure a perfect pronunciation & to make
a good Orator.

6 It is the oneley way to know where Nature hath bestowed the
benefit of a good voice: which gift is so rare, as there is not one
among a thousand that hath it: and in many, that excellent gift is
lost, because they want Art to express Nature.

7 There is not any Musicke of Instruments whatsoever, comparable
to that which is made of the voices of Men, where the voices are
good, and the same well sorted and ordered.

8 The better the voyce is, the meeter it is to honour and serve God
therewith: and the voyce of man is chiefely to be imployed to that
ende.

Omnis spiritus laudet Dominum.

Since singing is so good a thing
I wish all men would learn to sing.

*William Byrd (1543–1623),
from the Preface to 'Psalms, Sonnets and Songs', 1588*

7.7 Pilgrimage – Going Home

Tarry no longer; t'ward thine heritage
Haste on thy way, and be of right good cheer.
Go each day onward on thy pilgrimage;
Think how short time thou shalt abide here.
Thy place is bigg'd above the starres clear,
None earthly palace wrought in so stately wise.
Come on, my friend, my brother most entere!
For thee I offered my blood in sacrifice.

John Lydgate (c.1370-1447)

Jesus Christ the Apple Tree

The tree of life my soul hath seen,
Laden with fruit, and always green:
The trees of nature fruitless be
Compared with Christ the apple tree.

His beauty doth all things excel:
By faith I know, but ne'er can tell
The glory which I now can see
In Jesus Christ the apple tree.

For happiness I long have sought,
And pleasure dearly I have bought:
I missed of all; but now I see
'Tis found in Christ the apple tree.

I'm weary with my former toil,
Here I will sit and rest awhile:
Under the shadow I will be,
Of Jesus Christ the apple tree.

This fruit doth make my soul to thrive,
It keeps my dying faith alive;
Which makes my soul in haste to be
With Jesus Christ the apple tree.

Anon., collection of Joshua Smith, New Hampshire 1784

Give me my scallop-shell of quiet
My staff of faith to walk upon,
My scrip of joy, immortal diet,
My bottle of salvation,
My gown of glory, hope's true gage,
And thus I'll take my pilgrimage.

Sir Walter Raleigh (c.1552-1618)

A Gaelic blessing on beginning a journey:

Bless to me, O God,
    The earth beneath my foot;
Bless to me, O God,
    The path whereon I go;
Bless to me, O God,
    The thing of my desire;
        Thou Evermore of evermore,
    Bless Thou to me in my rest.

Bless to me the thing
    Whereon is set my mind;
Bless to me the thing
    Whereon is set my love;
Bless to me the thing
    Whereon is set my hope;
        O Thou King of kings
    Bless Thou to me mine eye.

O God, who hast brought us near to an innumerable company of
angels, and to the spirits of just men made perfect; grant us during our
earthly pilgrimage to abide in their fellowship, and in our heavenly
country to become partakers of their joy; through Jesus Christ our
Lord.

William Bright (1824-1901)

Alone with none but thee, my God
I journey on my way.
What need I fear, when thou art near
O king of night and day?
More safe am I within thy hand
Than if an host didst round me stand.

St Columba (c.521-597)

7.8 Love

Come, Holy Spirit, fill the hearts of your faithful people
and kindle in us the fire of your love.

Many waters cannot quench love,
neither can the floods drown it.

Song of Solomon 8.7

Love

Love bade me welcome: yet my soul drew back,
     Guiltie of dust and sinne.
But quick-ey'd Love, observing me grow slack
     From my first entrance in,
Drew nearer to me, sweetly questioning,
     If I lack'd any thing.

A guest, I answer'd, worthy to be here:
     Love said, you shall be he.
I the unkinde, ungratefull? Ah my deare,
     I cannot look on thee.
Love took my hand, and smiling did reply,
     Who made the eyes but I?

Truth Lord, but I have marr'd them: let my shame
     Go where it doth deserve.
And know you not, sayes Love, who bore the blame?
     My deare, then I will serve.
You must sit down, sayes Love, and taste my meat:
     So I did sit and eat.

George Herbert (1593-1633)

These are some of the many stanzas of a long hymn based on the account in Genesis 32.22–32 of Jacob wrestling with the unknown assailant in the night before he is to meet his brother Esau, whom he has wronged.

Come, O thou Traveller unknown,
Whom still I hold, but cannot see;
My company before is gone,
And I am left alone with thee;
With thee all night I mean to stay,
And wrestle till the break of day.

I need not tell thee who I am,
My misery or sin declare;
Thyself hast called me by my name;
Look on thy hands, and read it there!
But who, I ask thee, who art thou?
Tell me thy name, and tell me now.

In vain thou strugglest to get free;
I never will unloose my hold.
Art thou the man that died for me?
The secret of thy love unfold:
Wrestling, I will not let thee go,
Till I thy name, thy nature know.

Yield to me now, for I am weak,
But confident in self–despair;
Speak to my heart, in blessings speak,
To be conquered by my instant prayer.
Speak, or thou never hence shalt move,
And tell me if thy name is Love!

'Tis Love! 'tis Love! Thou diedst for me!
I hear thy whisper in my heart!
The morning breaks, the shadows flee;
Pure universal Love thou art:
To me, to all, thy mercies move;
Thy nature and thy name is Love.

Charles Wesley (1707–1788)

This hymn, for a long time part of the praying memory of Anglicans, has been given new life since it began to be sung to the fine Welsh tune, Blaenwaern.

Love divine, all loves excelling,
Joy of heaven, to earth come down,
Fix in us thy humble dwelling,
All thy faithful mercies crown.
Jesu, thou art all compassion,
Pure unbounded love thou art;
Visit us with thy salvation,
Enter every trembling heart.

Come, almighty to deliver,
Let us all thy grace receive;
Suddenly return, and never,
Never more thy temples leave.
Thee we would be always blessing,
Serve thee as thy hosts above;
Pray, and praise thee, without ceasing,
Glory in thy perfect love.

Finish then thy new creation:
Pure and spotless let us be;
Let us see thy great salvation
Perfectly restored in thee;
Changed from glory into glory
Till in heaven we take our place,
Till we cast our crowns before thee,
Lost in wonder, love, and praise.

Charles Wesley (1707-1788)

Come down, O Love divine,
seek thou this soul of mine,
and visit it with thine own ardour glowing;
O Comforter, draw near,
within my heart appear,
and kindle it, thy holy flame bestowing.

O let it freely burn,
till earthly passions turn
to dust and ashes in its heat consuming;
and let thy glorious light
shine ever on my sight,
and clothe me round, and while my path illuming.

Let holy charity
mine outward vesture be,
and lowliness become mine inner clothing:
True lowliness of heart,
which takes the humbler part,
and o'er its own shortcomings weeps with loathing.

And so the yearning strong,
with which the soul will long,
shall far outpass the power of human telling;
for none can guess its grace,
till he become the place
wherein the Holy Spirit makes his dwelling.

Bianco da Siena (d. 1434), tr. R. F. Littledale (1833-1890)

May the power of your love, Lord Christ,
fiery and sweet as honey,
so absorb our hearts
as to withdraw them from all that is under heaven.
Grant that we may be ready
to die for love of your love,
as you died for love of our love.

Franciscan

7.9 Prayers of Self Offering and Trusting

I bind unto myself today
The power of God to hold and lead,
His eye to watch, his might to stay,
His ear to hearken to my need.
The wisdom of my God to teach,
His hand to guide, his shield to ward;
The word of God to give me speech,
His heavenly host to be my guard.

From St Patrick's Breastplate

Be present, O merciful God,
and protect us through the silent hours of this night,
so that we who are wearied by the changes
    and chances of this fleeting world
may repose upon thy eternal changelessness;
through Jesus Christ our Lord.

Gelasian Sacramentary

O Lord Jesus Christ,
who created and redeemed me,
and hast brought unto that which I now am,
thou knowest what thou wouldst do with me;
do with me according to thy will,
for thy tender mercies sake.

King Henry VI (1421-1472)

Teach us, good Lord, to serve thee as thou deservest;
to give, and not to count the cost;
to fight, and not to heed the wounds;
to toil, and not to seek for rest;
to labour, and not to ask for any reward,
save that of knowing that we do thy will;
through Jesus Christ our Lord.

St Ignatius Loyola (1491-1556)

Eternal God,
the light of the minds that know thee,
the joy of the hearts that love thee
and the strength of the wills that serve thee;
grant us so to know thee that we may truly love thee,
so to love thee that we may truly serve thee,
whom to serve is perfect freedom;
through Jesus Christ our Lord.

Gelasian Sacramentary

7.10 For the Church and her Ministry

The Veni Creator is sung at the ordination of a priest or bishop

Come, Holy Ghost, our souls inspire,
And lighten with celestial fire;
Thou the anointing Spirit art,
Who dost thy sevenfold gifts impart:

Thy blessèd unction from above
Is comfort, life, and fire of love;
Enable with perpetual light
The dullness of our blinded sight:

Anoint and cheer our soilèd face
With the abundance of thy grace:
Keep far our foes, give peace at home;
Where thou art guide no ill can come.

Teach us to know the Father, Son,
And thee, of both, to be but One;
That through the ages all along
This may be our endless song,

Praise to thy eternal merit,
Father, Son, and Holy Spirit. Amen.

John Cosin (1594-1672)

A prayer for the Church:

Most gracious Father, we humbly pray
for your holy catholic Church:
fill it with all truth,
in all truth with all peace.
Where it is corrupt, purge it;
where it is in error, direct it;
where anything is amiss, reform it;
where it is right, strengthen and confirm it;
where it is in want, furnish it;
where it is divided and rent asunder,
make up the breaches of it,
O Holy One of Israel.   *William Laud (1573-1645)*

A prayer for mission and evangelism:

> Give to your Church, O God,
> a bold vision and a daring charity,
> a refreshed wisdom and a courteous understanding,
> the revival of her brightness and the renewal of her unity;
> that the eternal message of your Son,
> undefiled by the traditions of men
> may be acclaimed as the good news of the new age;
> through him who makes all things new,
> even Jesus Christ our Lord.

Percy Dearmer (1867-1936)

For faith, hope and charity:

> Lord God, heavenly Father,
> grant to your Church today
> the faith of her apostles,
> the hope of the martyrs
> and the love of her Lord,
> even Jesus Christ, in whose name we pray.

Christopher Idle (1938-)

7.11 For the Leaders of the Nations

Sovereign Lord of peoples and nations,
we pray for all who are called to leadership among their fellows;
give them vision to see far into the issues of their time,
courage to uphold what they believe to be right
    and integrity in their words and motives;
and may their service to their peoples promote the welfare and peace
    of the whole human race;
through Jesus Christ our Lord.

Basil Naylor (1911-1988)

O God, Almighty Father, King of kings and Lord of all rulers,
grant that the hearts and minds of all who go out as leaders before us,
the statesmen, the judges, the men of learning and the men of wealth,
may be so filled with the love of thy laws
    and of that which is righteous and lifegiving,
that they may serve as a wholesome salt unto the earth,
and be worthy stewards of thy good and perfect gifts;
through Jesus Christ our Lord.

Prayer of the Knights of the Garter

7.12 For Peace, Justice and Righteousness

Almighty God, from whom all thought of truth and peace proceed;
kindle, we pray thee, in the hearts of all men the true love of peace,
and guide with thy pure and peaceable wisdom
   those who take counsel for the nations of the earth;
that in tranquillity thy kingdom may go forward,
till the earth be filled with the knowledge of thy love;
through Jesus Christ our Lord.

Francis Paget (1851–1911)

O God, by your Son Jesus Christ you have set on earth
a kingdom of holiness to measure its strength against all others;
make faith to prevail over fear, and righteousness over force,
and truth over the lie, and love and concord over all things;
through Jesus Christ our Lord.

War Prayers 1940

God, the king of righteousness,
lead us, we pray, in the ways of justice and peace;
inspire us to break down all tyranny and oppression,
to gain for every person their due reward,
and from every person their due service;
that each may live for all,
and all may care for each,
in the name of Jesus Christ our Lord.

William Temple (1881–1944)

Lord, bless this kingdom and commonwealth,
that there may be peace and prosperity in all its borders.
In peace so preserve it that it corrupt not;
in trouble so defend it that it suffer not;
and so order it, whether in plenty or in want,
that it may faithfully serve you and patiently seek your kingdom,
the only sure foundation both of men and states;
through Jesus Christ our saviour and Redeemer.

After William Laud (1573–1645)

7.13 For the Sick or Suffering, and for the Weak

Watch thou, O Lord, with those who wake, or watch,
   or weep tonight,
and give thine angels charge over those who sleep.
Tend the sick, rest the weary, bless the dying,
soothe the suffering, pity the afflicted, shield the joyous,
and all for thy love's sake.

St Augustine (354-430)

God of love, whose compassion never fails;
we bring before you the griefs and perils of peoples and nations;
the necessities of the homeless; the helplessness of the aged and weak;
the sighings of prisoners; the pains of the sick and injured;
   the sorrow of the bereaved.
Comfort and relieve them, O merciful Father, according
   to their needs;
for the sake of your Son, our Saviour Jesus Christ.

After St Anselm (1033-1109)

Almighty and everlasting God,
the comfort of the sad, the strength of those who suffer;
hear the prayers of your children who cry out of any tribulation;
and to every soul that is distressed, grant mercy, relief and refreshment;
through Jesus Christ our Lord.

Gelasian Sacramentary

7.14 Well-Known Prayers

O God, forasmuch as without thee we are not able to please thee;
Mercifully grant that thy Holy Spirit may in all things direct and rule
our hearts; through Jesus Christ our Lord.

Collect for the 19th Sunday after Trinity
The Book of Common Prayer

Almighty God, who hast given us grace at this time with one accord
to make our common supplications unto thee; and dost promise, that
when two or three are gathered together in thy Name thou wilt grant
their requests: Fulfil now, O Lord, the desires and petitions of thy
servants, as may be most expedient for them; granting us in this world
knowledge of thy truth, and in the world to come life everlasting.

St John Chrysostom (349-407)
The Book of Common Prayer

Steer the ship of my life, good Lord, to your quiet harbour,
where I can be safe from the storms of sin and conflict.
Show me the course that I should steer.
Renew in me the gift of discernment,
so that I can always see the right path in which I should go.
And give me the strength and courage to choose the right course
even when the sea is rough and the waves are high,
knowing that through enduring hardship and danger
we shall find comfort and peace.

St Basil of Caesarea (c.330-379)

Late have I loved Thee, O Beauty both so ancient and so new,
yea, too late I came to love thee;
for behold, Thou wert within me, and I outside;
and I sought Thee outside
and in my unloveliness fell upon those lovely things that Thou
hast made.
Thou wert with me, and I was not with Thee.
I was kept from Thee by those things,
yet had they not been in Thee, they would have not been at all.
Thou didst call and cry to me to break open my deafness;
Thou didst send forth thy beams
and shine upon me and chase away my blindness.
Thou didst breathe fragrance upon me,
and I drew in my breath and do now pant for Thee.
I tasted Thee, and now hunger and thirst for Thee;
Thou didst touch me, and I ever burn again to enjoy Thy peace.

St Augustine (354-430)

O God, from whom to be turned is to fall,
to whom to be turned is to rise,
and in whom to stand is to abide for ever;
grant us in all our duties your help,
in all our perplexities your guidance,
in all our dangers your protection,
and in all our sorrows your peace;
through Jesus Christ, our Lord.

St Augustine (354-430)

Almighty God, in whom we live and move and have our being,
thou hast made us for thyself, and our hearts are restless till they find
their rest in thee;
grant us such purity of heart and strength of purpose,
that no selfish passion may hinder us from knowing thy will,
and no weakness from doing it;
but that in thy light we may see light,
and in thy service find perfect freedom;
through Jesus Christ our Lord.

St Augustine (354-430)

Thanks be to thee, O Lord Jesus Christ,
for all the benefits which thou hast won for us,
for all the pains and insults thou hast borne for us.
O most merciful Redeemer, Friend and Brother,
may I know thee more clearly,
love thee more dearly
and follow thee more nearly
day by day.

Attributed to St Richard of Chichester (1253)

Lord, make me an instrument of your peace.
Where there is hatred, let me sow love;
where there is injury, pardon;
where there is doubt, faith;
where there is despair, hope;
where there is darkness, light;
where there is sadness, joy.
O Divine Master, grant that I may not so much
seek to be consoled as to console,
to be understood as to understand,
to be loved as to love.
For it is in giving that we receive,
it is in pardoning that we are pardoned,
and it is in dying that we are born to eternal life.

19th century French prayer

Nada de turba

Let nothing disturb you,
Nothing dismay you;
All things are passing:
God never changes.
Patient endurance
Attains all that it strives for;
Those who have God
Find they lack nothing.
God alone suffices.

St Teresa of Avila (1515-1582) – her bookmark

Eternal and most glorious God, who hast stamped the soul of man with thine image, received it into thy Revenue, and made it a part of thy Treasure; suffer us not so to undervalue ourselves, nay, so to impoverish thee, as to give away these souls for nothing, and all the world is nothing if the soul must be given for it. Do this, O God, for his sake who knows our natural infirmities, for he had them, and knows the weight of our sins, for he paid a dear price for them, thy Son our Saviour Jesus Christ.

From the peroration of a sermon by John Donne (1572-1631)

Christ be with me, Christ within me,
Christ behind me, Christ before me,
Christ beside me, Christ to win me,
Christ to comfort and restore me.
Christ beneath me, Christ above me,
Christ in quiet, Christ in danger,
Christ in hearts of all who love me,
Christ in mouth of friend and stranger.

From St Patrick's Breastplate

Grant, Lord,
that we may hold to you without parting
worship you without wearying, serve you without failing;
faithfully seek you, happily find you and for ever possess you,
the only God, blessed, now and for ever.

St Anselm (1033-1109)

Eternal light, shine into our hearts,
Eternal Goodness, deliver us from evil,
Eternal Power, be our support,
Eternal Wisdom, scatter the darkness of our ignorance,
Eternal Pity, have mercy upon us;
that with all our heart and mind and soul and strength
we may seek thy face
and be brought by thy infinite mercy to thy holy presence;
through Jesus Christ our Lord.

Alcuin of York (735-804)

Into thy hand, O Father and Lord, we commend our souls
    and bodies,
our parents and our homes, friends and servants, neighbours
    and kindred,
our benefactors and brethren departed, all folk rightly believing
and all who need thy pity and protection.
Light us with thy holy grace
and suffer us never to be separated from thee,
O Lord in Trinity, God everlasting.

St Edmund of Abingdon (1170-1240)

Give me, O Lord, a steadfast heart that no unworthy thought
    can diminish;
give me an unconquered heart that no tribulation can sap;
give me an upright heart that no base purpose can seduce.
Bestow on me also, O Lord our God,
understanding to know you,
persistence to seek you,
wisdom to find you
and a faithfulness which may at the end embrace you;
through Jesus Christ our Lord.

St Thomas Aquinas (1225-1274)

Gracious and holy Father,
give us wisdom to perceive you,
diligence to seek you,
patience to wait for you,
eyes to behold you,
a heart to meditate on you,
and a life to proclaim you;
through the power of the Spirit of Jesus Christ, our Lord.

St Benedict (c.480-543)

Grant us, O Lord, to know that which is worth knowing,
to love that which is worth loving,
to praise that which is pleasing to thee,
to value that which is most precious to thee,
and to hate whatever is evil in thy sight.
Suffer us not to judge according to our senses,
but to discern with true judgement between things spiritual
    and temporal,
and above all to search out and to do what is well-pleasing unto thee;
through Jesus Christ our Lord.

Thomas à Kempis (1379-1471)

Grant us, O Lord, not to set our hearts on earthly things, but to love
    things heavenly;
and even now, while we are set among things that are passing away,
to cleave unto those that shall abide; through Jesus Christ our Lord.

Leonine Sacramentary

O Lord God, when thou givest to thy servants to endeavour any
    great matter,
grant us to know that it is not the beginning but the continuing
    of the same,
until it be thoroughly finished, which yieldeth the true glory;
through him who, for the finishing of thy work, laid down his life
    for us,
even our Redeemer, Jesus Christ.

Eric Milner-White, based on the prayer of
Sir Francis Drake (1540-1596) as he sailed into Cadiz

O Lord our heavenly Father,
Almighty and everlasting God,
who hast safely brought us to the beginning of this day;
Defend us in the same with thy mighty power;
and grant that this day we fall into no sin,
neither run into any kind of danger;
but that all our doings may be ordered by thy governance,
to do always that is righteous in thy sight;
through Jesus Christ our Lord.

The Third Collect at Morning Prayer, The Book of Common Prayer

Bring us, O Lord God, at our last awakening into the house
and gate of heaven,
to enter into that gate and dwell in that house,
where there shall be no darkness nor dazzling, but one equal light;
no noise nor silence, but one equal music;
no fears nor hopes, but one equal possession;
no ends nor beginnings, but one equal eternity;
in the habitations of thy glory and dominion,
world without end.

After John Donne (1571-1631)

Remember, O Lord, what thou hast wrought in us and not
what we deserve;
and as thou hast called us to thy service, make us worthy of
our calling;
through Jesus Christ our Lord.

The Prayer Book as proposed in 1928

O God, who hast prepared for them that love thee such good things as
pass man's understanding; pour into our hearts such love toward thee,
that we, loving thee above all things, may obtain thy promises, which
exceed all that we can desire; through Jesus Christ our Lord.

Collect for the Sixth Sunday after Trinity,
The Book of Common Prayer

Grant, Lord, that we may live in your fear,
die in your favour, rest in your peace,
rise in your power and reign in your glory;
for your own beloved Son's sake,
Jesus Christ our Lord.

William Laud (1573-1645)

O Saviour of the world, who by thy Cross and precious blood
hast redeemed us;
save us and help us we humbly beseech thee, O Lord.

The Prayer Book as proposed in 1928

God grant to the living, grace; to the departed, rest; to the Church,
the Queen, the commonwealth and all mankind, peace and concord;
and to us and all his servants life everlasting.

Based on a 16th century prayer

Ye holy angels bright,
Who wait at God's right hand,
Or through the realms of light
Fly at your Lord's command,
Assist our song,
For else the theme
Too high doth seem
For mortal tongue.

Ye blessed souls at rest,
Who ran this earthly race,
And now, from sin released,
Behold the Saviour's face,
God's praises sound,
As in his sight
With sweet delight
Ye do abound.

Ye saints, who toil below,
Adore your heavenly King.
And onward as ye go
Some joyful anthem sing;
Take what he gives
And praise him still,
Through good or ill,
Who ever lives!

My soul, bear thou thy part,
Triumph in God above:
And with a well-tuned heart
Sing thou the songs of love!
Let all thy days
Till life shall end,
Whate'er he send,
Be filled with praise

Richard Baxter (1615-1691)

8   A Coda: Quick Prayers

There are many phrases, short sayings and prayers which have become part of the currency of Christian prayer. These are some examples, both from the Bible and from the tradition. They can be ways of recalling God's presence on a busy day, or reminding you of St Paul's encouragement to 'pray at all times'.

> Prayer is
> The world in tune.
>
> *Henry Vaughan (1622-1695)*

From the Bible

Not unto us, O Lord, not unto us but to your name give the glory.
From Psalm 115

Speak, Lord, for your servant hears.
The child Samuel, as instructed by Eli (1 Samuel 3.10)

Lord, I believe; help thou my unbelief.
The father of the deaf-mute's cry (Mark 9.24)

God, be merciful to me, a sinner.
Prayer of the tax collector in the temple (Luke 18.13)

Have mercy on me, O God, in your great goodness;
Wash me from my wickedness and cleanse me from my sin.
From Psalm 51: Miserere

My Lord and my God.
St Thomas, as he met the risen Christ himself (John 20.28)

Father, not my will but thine be done.
Jesus' prayer in the garden of Gethsemane (Mark 14.36)

Father, into your hands I commend my spirit.
From Psalm 31, quoted by Jesus on the cross in Luke's Gospel (Luke 23.46)

Jesus, remember me when you come into your Kingdom.
The penitent thief to Jesus on the cross (Luke 23.42)

Maranatha: Come, Lord Jesus.
1 Corinthians 16.22 and the Revelation to John (22.20)
— a prayer of the early Church

O Lord, thou knowest how busy I must be this day.
If I forget thee, do not thou forget me.

Sir Jacob Astley, before the battle of Edgehill

God give me work
Till my life shall end
And life
Till my work is done.

On the gravestone of Winifred Holtby (1898-1935)

Jesu mercy, Mary pray.

Traditional inscription on a grave marker

Here, Lord, is my life:
I place it on the altar today.
Use it as you will.

Albert Schweitzer (1875-1965)

God grant me
serenity to accept the things I cannot change,
courage to change the things I can,
and the wisdom to know the difference.

Attributed to Reinhold Niebuhr (1892-1971)

O God,
Help us not to despise or oppose
What we do not understand.

William Penn (1644-1718)

Lord, give us faith that right makes might.

Abraham Lincoln (1809-1865)

O Lord, let us not live to be useless, for Christ's sake.

John Wesley (1703-1791)

These things, good Lord, that we pray for,
Give us thy grace to labour for.

Sir Thomas More (1478-1535)

Thou who hast given so much to me
Give one thing more, a grateful heart.

George Herbert (1593-1633)

Lord, let thy glory be my end,
thy word my rule
and then thy will be done.

King Charles I (1600-1649)

For all that has been – Thanks!
For all that shall be – Yes!

Dag Hammarskjöld (1905-1961)

Protégéz moi, mon Seigneur;
Ma barque est si petite,
Et votre mer est si grande.

Protect me, O Lord;
My boat is so small
And your sea so big.

An old Breton fisherman's prayer

God be in my head,
and in my understanding;
God be in myne eyes
and in my looking;
God be in my mouth
and in my speaking;
God be in myne heart
and in my thinking;
God be at my end
and at my departing.

From a Sarum Primer (1514)

Acknowledgements

For permission to reproduce the following material, the publishers would like to thank:

Faber and Faber for permission to reproduce *Journey of the Magi*, an extract from *Little Gidding*, and an extract from *East Coker* by T. S. Eliot

John Murray (Publishers) Ltd for permission to reproduce *Classical Landscape with Figures* by Osbert Lancaster

Perpetua Press, Oxford, and the translator for permission to reproduce *I saw him standing*, by Ann Griffiths, tr. Rowan Williams

B. Thomas for permission to reproduce the poems by R. S. Thomas

Every effort has been made to contact the copyright holders of material featured in this book. The publishers welcome any queries from those copyright holders we have been unable to contact.